Exploring the World of Animals

Literature Bridges to Science Series

The World of Water: Linking Fiction to Nonfiction. By Phyllis J. Perry. 1995

The World's Regions and Weather: Linking Fiction to Nonfiction. By Phyllis J. Perry. 1996

Rainy, Windy, Snowy, Sunny Days: Linking Fiction to Nonfiction. By Phyllis J. Perry. 1996

Exploring the World of Animals: Linking Fiction to Nonfiction. By Phyllis J. Perry. 1997

Exploring the World of Animals

Linking Fiction to Nonfiction

Phyllis J. Perry

TEACHER IDEAS PRESS
A Division of
Libraries Unlimited, Inc.
Englewood, Colorado
1997

TEACHER IDEAS PRESS
A Division of
Libraries Unlimited, Inc.
P.O. Box 6633
Englewood, CO 80155-6633
1-800-237-6124

Production Editor: Kevin W. Perizzolo
Copy Editor: Curtis D. Holmes
Proofreader: Shannon Graff
Typesetter: Kay Minnis

Library of Congress Cataloging-in-Publication Data

Perry, Phyllis Jean.
    Exploring the world of animals : linking fiction to nonfiction /
by Phyllis J. Perry.
      xvii, 133 p. 22x28 cm. -- (Literature bridges to science series)
    Includes bibliographical references (p. 121) and index.
    ISBN 1-56308-517-8
    1. Animals--Study and teaching (Elementary) 2. Animals--Juvenile
fiction--Bibliography. 3. Animals--Juvenile literature--
Bibliography. 4. Interdisciplinary approach in education.
I. Title. II. Series.
QL51.P47   1997
372.3'5--dc21   96-39100
                                                   CIP

For
Clare Marie Miller
whose clear vision and love of animals is revealed in her art,
which appears as separation pages in this book.

Contents

Part I
Animals at Home

**Part II
Animals on the Farm**

**Part III
Animals in the Woods**

Part IV
Animals in the Wild

Part V
Additional Resources

About the Series

In the era of literature-based reading programs, students are involved in narrative texts more than ever, but they still face difficulty when confronted with expository text. Many experts believe that one of the best ways to teach a subject is to *engage* the learner, that is, to get the student so interested in a topic that the motivation to learn increases.

The Literature Bridges to Science series uses the power of fictional works to lead students from the world of imagination into the world of fact. In this series, fiction is used to build interest, increase familiarity with a topic, enlarge background knowledge, and introduce vocabulary. The fiction is intended to be enjoyed, letting the power of the stories increase the desire to learn more about a topic. Several fictional works are used, which suit both individual tastes and the breadth of experience in a group of students.

As student interest builds, two "bridge" titles are used to pique interest. At this point, confident that the learners are not starting at ground zero in their background knowledge, the teacher(s) can introduce a main theme of study. Interest in the topic might then be high enough to motivate students to attack the expository writing in works of nonfiction.

Just as several fictional works are used to introduce a topic, the Literature Bridges to Science series suggests that numerous nonfiction works be offered to students as they begin their topical explorations. The series is particularly useful to teachers who are transforming their teaching style to a cross-curricular content approach. Nonfiction titles are chosen carefully to represent the more literary treatment of a topic in contrast to a textbook-like stream of facts. A collection of poetry is also included in each section to broaden the reading options.

Introduction

This book is designed to assist busy elementary teachers who are planning a unit of study about animals. It includes suggestions for individual, small-, and large-group activities across the disciplines. A range of titles allows for student choice based on interest and skill level. Some are picture books that kindergarten students will enjoy, while others provide challenging reading for fifth-grade students. The titles were selected from a large number of books recommended by children's librarians.

Between the fiction and nonfiction books in each section are two books that are suggested to serve as "bridges." The bridges combine factual information and fictional elements. This blend of fact and fiction enables the reader to make an easy transition from one type of material to another. A suggested poetry collection is also included for each section.

Parts I, II, III, and IV begin with summaries of fiction books, with discussion starters and suggested multidisciplinary activities following each summary. Next are summaries of related nonfiction books of various lengths and levels of difficulty with suggested topics for further investigation following each summary. The suggested activities involve skills in research, oral and written language, science, math, geography, and the arts.

Each part begins with a "bookweb" suggesting ideas for discussion and projects that might come out of the fiction, bridges, poetry, and nonfiction materials. All of the suggested books were published since 1980 and most since 1990, so they are readily available. They represent many cultures and eras and include folktales and legends as well as contemporary material.

📖 Teaching Methods 📖

One Teacher with Multiple Teaching Responsibilities

In most cases at the elementary level, a single teacher is responsible for teaching a variety of subjects to a group of students. If the same teacher is responsible for teaching language arts, social studies, math, and science, the cross-curricular approach suggested here will have a unifying effect on the curricula.

Before beginning a unit on animals, the teacher might, for example, present one of the fiction books as a read-aloud in class. This helps to set the tone for the upcoming unit of study. As they hear a good piece of literature featuring an animal or group of animals, students will begin to learn vocabulary, and to focus on animals at home, on the farm, in the woods, and in the wild.

The teacher might suggest that students be alert to information about endangered animals. Students might be encouraged to bring articles clipped from newspapers and magazines for a classroom vertical file. If a television special is scheduled that focuses on some aspect of animal life, the teacher or another student could alert the class to the opportunity for viewing, or, with permission, might tape it to share in class.

Once the unit begins, the teacher might have each student select one of the fiction titles in part I and encourage small-group discussion among those who have read the same book. This extends reading and listening skills, and the use of oral language.

The teacher may want to use the bridge books to assist those who may not feel as comfortable with nonfiction as with fiction. Since the bridge books combine elements of a story or real-life adventure with information and facts, students are assisted in moving from one type of reading to another. Their growing vocabulary and knowledge about the world of animals from the fiction works will be assets for reading, understanding, and appreciating nonfiction.

The teacher might assign writing topics concerning animals and may combine these with a science assignment. In this way, a student studying snow leopards, for example, will do library research and, where appropriate, prepare a bibliography and have practice writing an informative paper.

In a creative writing assignment, the student might write an original short story based on a day on a farm. This would be an excellent time to use poetry related to animals. A collection of poetry is included in each of the four major sections of the book. Students may read poems and experiment with writing their own.

The teacher might also select books combining social studies and geography as students learn more about animals that live in the rain forest, or the special animals found in Australia, or adaptations that animals make to survive in the Arctic.

Departmentalization with Team Planning

In schools where there is departmentalization but team planning time, the language arts, social studies, and science teachers can plan a unit on animals. The science teacher may concentrate on habitats and environments. The social studies teacher can use the unit to discuss the tropics, Arctic or Antarctic, to concentrate on reading and making maps, using legends, computing distances on maps, etc.

The language arts teacher can concentrate on reading, research, and writing assignments using both the fiction and nonfiction books. Panel discussions and oral presentation of material allow practice of speaking and listening skills, as do the suggestions for puppet shows and dramatic presentations. Specific skills such as skimming, reading for information, note taking, outlining, or using an index or a glossary of terms might also be introduced or reinforced using the suggested nonfiction books.

Some students will find it easy to process information presented in the nonfiction books in graphs, charts, and pictures. For others, these may be confusing or novel sources of information. The teacher can explain how to "read" these special materials and may make assignments to provide students an opportunity to construct charts and graphs.

Specialists might also be involved. The music teacher may incorporate songs involving animals, while the art teacher might use mobiles, collages, clay models of animals, etc. Classroom and hall bulletin boards might feature a section on endangered species or announce the times and dates of a new exhibit in a natural history museum.

If a computer lab is available, materials dealing with animals, such as food chains and animal camouflage could be highlighted. Students might also use the computer stations to compose their own written reports.

If the media specialist is responsible for teaching research skills to students, the focus may be on using an encyclopedia or CD-ROM that features a specific food chain, using a vertical file to research animals of the rain forest, or doing a computer search on animals of the Arctic. The media specialist may highlight those magazines and books in the collection that deal with animals, and might even do some interlibrary loans to increase available materials during the unit of study.

Team Teaching

In schools with team teaching, team members can choose to present their favorite lessons and experiments. They may choose from personal strengths or from an interest to learn more about a topic. Next, teachers can map out a sequence and time line so that their students will see the connections between subject areas.

While one teacher is presenting a lesson, colleagues can assist by being part of small-group discussions, providing assistance with science experiments, or supervising a group of students in the media center who might be involved in small-group or individual research.

Some activities in a team-teaching situation can be presented to a large group of students. Showing films or videos falls into this category. Team members can then be responsible for work stations or break-out groups where smaller numbers of students will have the opportunity to extend their knowledge.

📖 Culminating Activities 📖

Whatever the configuration of students and teachers, there might well be an opportunity for a special culminating activity for each part. Part I, for example, deals with animals at home. The students could be assembled in a gym for a special demonstration given by a local dog trainer. The trainer could explain what dogs learn during obedience training and how this training can make the dog easier to keep at home, as well as a better companion when walking in the woods, or when traveling.

As an example of a culminating activity for part III, animals in the woods, each student might be responsible for adding a food chain to be placed in an enormous food web of the woods to be hung on a large bulletin board. When the web is complete, individual students could present their food chains and discuss the interrelationships of the various food chains to one another.

📖 Scope and Sequence 📖

Part I covers animals at home. The fiction books include picture books and chapter books. Each book deals with a common household pet. The nonfiction books are also related to the selection and care of common and more exotic pets in the home or yard.

Part II deals with animals that live on farms. The fiction books include picture books and chapter books. The nonfiction books are related to farming, ranching, the work of large-animal veterinarians, and types of farm animals.

Part III concerns animals in the woods. The fiction books include picture books and chapter books. The nonfiction books provide information to help students understand how human population increases and the growth of towns and cities have effected the habitat of common woodland animals.

Part IV involves animals in the wild. The fiction books include picture books and chapter books. The nonfiction books deal with topics such as endangered species, loss of rain forests, game preserves, etc.

Part V is a list of additional resources. There are listings of other fiction and nonfiction books for each of the four major parts—animals at home, on the farm, in the woods, and in the wild—and some suggestions for magazines and videos that might be of interest.

Part I
Animals at Home

Animals at Home

● FICTION ●

- 📖 *Arthur's New Puppy*
- 📖 *The Cat Next Door*
- 📖 *The Junkyard Dog*
- 📖 *Martha Speaks*
- 📖 *Max and Minnie*
- 📖 *Mrs. Peachtree and the Eighth Avenue Cat*

- 📖 *Out of Nowhere*
- 📖 *A Question of Trust*
- 📖 *Shiloh*
- 📖 *Sophie in the Saddle*
- 📖 *Windsong*

◆ BRIDGES AND POETRY ◆

- 📖 *I Am the Dog, I Am the Cat*
- 📖 *I Love Guinea Pigs*
- 📖 *Cats Are Cats*

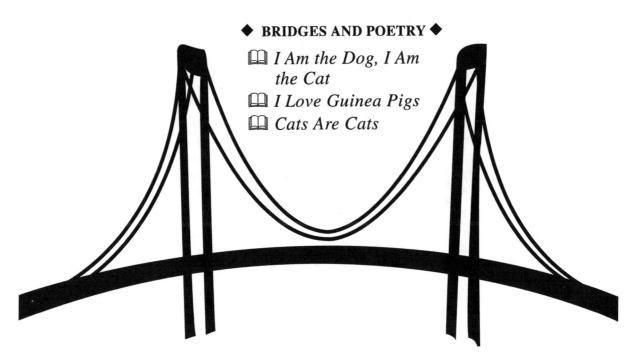

■ NONFICTION CONNECTIONS ■

- 📖 *Gerbils*
- 📖 *Hedgehogs: How to Take Care of Them and Understand Them*
- 📖 *Helping Our Animal Friends*
- 📖 *How to Look After Your Rabbit*
- 📖 *Kitten Care and Critters, Too!*

- 📖 *Patrol Dogs: Keeping the Peace*
- 📖 *The Pets You Love*
- 📖 *A Puppy Is Born*
- 📖 *Rosie, A Visiting Dog's Story*
- 📖 *Taking Care of Your Dog*
- 📖 *Why Mammals Have Fur*

—OTHER TOPICS TO EXPLORE—

—AKC	—ASPCA	—pet grooming	—sled dogs
—ant farms	—canaries	—rabies	—tropical fish
—aquariums	—greyhound racing	—sheep dogs	—vivariums

● *Fiction* ●

  📖 *Arthur's New Puppy*

  📖 *The Cat Next Door*

  📖 *The Junkyard Dog*

  📖 *Martha Speaks*

  📖 *Max and Minnie*

  📖 *Mrs. Peachtree and the Eighth Avenue Cat*

  📖 *Out of Nowhere*

  📖 *A Question of Trust*

  📖 *Shiloh*

  📖 *Sophie in the Saddle*

  📖 *Windsong*

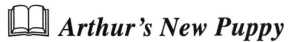 # Arthur's New Puppy

FICTION

by Marc Brown
Boston: Little, Brown, 1993. 32p.

This picture book has colorful illustrations with about six lines of text per page. It will appeal to readers in the primary grades. *Arthur's New Puppy* is the eighteenth book in the bestselling Arthur Adventure series.

Arthur has a new and very active puppy named Pal. When he takes Pal to the garage and explains that this will be Pal's new home, Pal hides and seems to be lonesome. Arthur persuades his mother to let Pal stay in the house for a day or two.

In the kitchen, Pal leaves a puddle of "excitement" in Arthur's lap. Yet, Arthur is not upset and explains that Pal is just a baby. After Pal eats, Arthur tries to take him outside on his leash, but Pal hides. Now there's another puddle on the rug! That night, Pal yelps and howls and wakes up the whole family.

The next morning, Pal has made a mess of the kitchen and living room. Pal has destroyed the drapes and D. W.'s doll.

Father puts the key to the garage on the hall table and announces that he will help move the puppy back there after dinner. But when Arthur goes to get the key, it is gone, so Pal spends another night in the house.

Arthur sets up a training school in the backyard. By the end of the week Pal will come, sit, and do a trick. Everyone is impressed and says Pal can stay inside, so Pal returns the garage key he has hidden behind a bush. That night, when Arthur tries to take Pal for a walk, the leash is gone. Arthur has hidden it.

Discussion Starters and Multidisciplinary Activities

1 Ask students if they had guessed what would happen early in the story when Arthur decided to spend the first night with his crying puppy. Did they think Arthur would remember to shut the gate, or did they think Pal would get out and cause mischief?

2 Encourage students to explain what they thought had happened to the garage key that Arthur's father had put on the table. Did anyone guess, before reading the end of the story, that Pal had hidden the key outside?

3 Invite students to share their own stories about what happened when a new puppy or kitten came to their house. Did some students have the same kinds of problems that Arthur had?

4 When the story ends, Pal has only been with his new family for a week. Although he has learned to obey some commands, more problems with the puppy are likely. Ask students to write another episode to the story in which Pal gets involved in a new problem. Share these with the class.

5 Arthur and his family members are aardvarks. Ask a pair of interested students to research more about aardvarks. Where do they live? What do they look like? What do they eat? Allow these students to share their information orally.

6 If someone nearby teaches dog obedience classes, invite that person to visit and explain how to train a puppy. Ask pupils to follow up with a thank-you note and to tell something they learned from the visit.

From *Exploring the World of Animals*. © 1997. Teacher Ideas Press. (800) 237-6124.

📖 *The Cat Next Door*

FICTION

by Betty Ren Wright
Illustrated by Gail Owens
New York: Holiday House, 1991. 32p.

This picture book has lovely, soft pastel illustrations appealing to readers in the primary grades. It is in the first person from a young girl's viewpoint.

Each summer, a girl and her parents drive to a cabin that Grandma and Grandpa own at a lake. As soon as she arrives, the young girl always runs down to the boat dock where she sits in the sun and listens to the gulls. She peeks through the slatted boards to see the water underneath.

Grandma comes and sits down beside her on the boat dock. They don't have to wait long before the cat next door comes to meow in the girl's ear. Each morning of the vacation the cat comes out to the dock to greet the girl.

During past summers, the girl floated on a raft with Grandma and they had picnics at the end of the dock. In the evening, Grandpa would take the girl and Grandma for a boat ride to see the ducks and gulls. Grandma said each day would last forever because that's how long they are going to remember it.

This year is different because Grandma has died. But the family returns to the cabin to keep Grandpa company. The young girl walks out to the dock. She misses her Grandma and begins to cry. Then the cat next door appears with two kittens. The girl laughs out loud and says hello to the kittens. She knows her grandmother would have loved this special surprise, too.

Discussion Starters and Multidisciplinary Activities

1 No one in this story has a name. What reasons might an author have for not naming characters? Ask students what names they would choose for the girl, the cat next door, the two kittens, Grandma, and Grandpa.

2 Encourage students to share special times they may have spent with an older relative. Where did they go, and what did they do?

3 The cat next door did not seem to pay attention to anyone except the young girl. Ask readers why they think the cat was so fond of this girl who came every summer?

4 Many music shops sell tapes that include the sounds of waves and the call of gulls. Ask a pair of students to find background music that they think fits this story. Play it for the class.

5 All sea gulls are not the same. With a little research, you can learn to identify several of the common gulls by the presence or absence of rings around the beak, the color of feet, etc. Ask a pair of students to do research on sea gulls. Have them share pictures, explaining how you can tell one gull from another.

6 The reader does not know the lake or state where this story takes place. Have students plan a trip to a lake in your state. Find out the following: the lake's depth, width, and how many miles it is to drive round trip to the lake?

📖 *The Junkyard Dog*

FICTION

by Erika Tamar
New York: Alfred A. Knopf, 1995. 185p.

Third- through fifth-grade readers will enjoy this contemporary story set in the city and told from the viewpoint of a fifth-grade girl, Katie Lawrence.

Katie lives with her mother and her mother's new husband, Jim Grady, in a group of very small houses near the waterfront. Katie resents Jim.

In this story, Crystal is Katie's best friend, but Katie is uneasy about a new girl at school, Damita, who seems to be taking up too much of Crystal's time. Damita likes makeup and boys.

As the story opens, Katie sees some teenagers teasing a junkyard dog, and tries to help it. She begins taking food and water to the dog daily. Although Katie's mother opposes this, Jim Grady supports Katie and tries to help her with her mission to aid the dog, which she names Lucky. Jim Grady encourages her to talk with the junkyard owner, Mr. Farrow, to get permission to feed the dog. Later Jim helps and encourages her in her efforts to build a doghouse for Lucky.

Damita has a party, to which she invites both boys and girls. The party is almost a disaster. It does show Katie that Daniel, a boy Katie likes, has many good points, and later, Daniel helps Katie finish building the doghouse. Jim Grady says they will be moving into a better home next spring and that Katie can have Lucky live with them then. Katie accepts Jim as her father and looks forward to a new home, a better life with Lucky, and keeping Daniel for a friend.

Discussion Starters and Multidisciplinary Activities

1   Although Jim Grady says that he is not used to having a daughter, in many ways he helps Katie deal with her problems more effectively than Katie's mother. Have students discuss some of the ways Jim shows that he is ready to be a good father.

2   Katie is upset when Daniel ignores her at school. She finally confronts him, sharing her feelings about this. Daniel says he ignores her at school so they will not be teased. Have students discuss teasing.

3   Jim Grady tells Katie that she must speak up and tell adults what she wants if she is going to deal effectively with people. Have students share experiences discussing matters with adults outside their family.

4   The author wrote this book after learning about Chitra Besbroda, a psychotherapist living in New York City, who has gained national attention for her work with abused animals. Have a pair of interested students work with a media specialist to learn more about Chitra Besbroda and share this information.

5   A small group of students might want to find out more about a tax-exempt animal charity, The Sentient Creatures, Inc., P.O. Box 765, Cathedral Station, New York, NY 10025. If they find it worthy, they may want to sponsor a small fund-raiser and devote the profits to this or a similar cause.

6   One or more students might enjoy making an illustration, using any medium, showing a cleaned-up Lucky at his new home, with Katie.

FICTION

📖 *Martha Speaks* E M467m

by Susan Meddaugh
Boston: Houghton Mifflin, 1992. 32p.

This picture book with its humorous and colorful line drawings will be enjoyed by primary grade readers.

As the book begins, Helen feeds alphabet soup to her dog, Martha. Instead of just going down into the dog's stomach, the letters seem to go up into Martha's brain. The dog can now speak, asking and answering questions. Everyone is amazed.

But there are some problems with owning a dog that can talk. For one thing, the dog learns to use the telephone. Martha calls Acme Meat and places an order. She also sometimes startles people outside the family, such as the pizza delivery man, when she speaks to them.

Martha speaks her mind and always tells the truth, which sometimes embarrasses the family members. Martha talks constantly and tells anyone who will listen the plots of TV shows. Everyone gets so upset with Martha's constant talking, that they finally tell her to shut up.

Martha is deeply offended. She refuses to eat her soup and stops talking. One night a burglar comes. Martha tries dialing 911, but can only bark. In the kitchen, the burglar gives Martha some soup to keep her quiet. The alphabet soup restores her ability to talk, so Martha calls 911. By the time family members return home, the police are there.

The family now heaps praise on Martha and tries to help her learn when to talk and when to be quiet.

Discussion Starters and Multidisciplinary Activities

1 Ask students to discuss whether they would like to have their own cat or dog start to speak. What would be the advantages? The disadvantages?

2 Have students tell who they think their pet would call if it were able to speak. Why?

3 Martha sulks and stops talking during the story. Later, she begins speaking again. Do you think that the family will be able to teach Martha when she should speak and when she should be quiet?

4 Drawing balloons over a character's head in a story indicates dialogue. Ask students to draw several panels for an original comic strip and put dialogue in balloons. Include a dog in the comic strip. Allow time to share these cartoons.

5 Learning how to use 911 in an emergency is important. Spend time with the class role playing. Have one student be a police dispatcher, while another child plays a person calling for help from a burning home. What information should be given over the phone?

6 Burglaries often occur in homes while the occupants are away for a holiday or vacation. Discuss and review some things that reduce the possibility of burglary. (Stop the newspaper, have the post office hold the mail, leave a timed light in the house, alert a neighbor to your absence, etc.)

 *Max and Minnie*

FICTION

by Catherine Walters
New York: Peter Bedrick Books, 1992. 32p.

This picture book with colorful illustrations will appeal to students in kindergarten through second grade. The settings for the book show both the comfort of a home and some dangers of venturing into the woods.

The story begins on a cold winter night as Max and Minnie are dozing by the fire. The cats awake hearing a little scratching noise, as if an animal is running across the floor. They chase a mouse behind the couch and stop at the mouse hole. Suddenly things change. The magic mouse hole is now large enough for the cats to enter.

After they step through the mouse hole, Max and Minnie find themselves surrounded by trees in a windy woods. All around them shine the eyes of creatures they have only dreamed of—mice, voles, rats, shrews, rabbits, birds, and squirrels.

Max chases a squirrel. Minnie catches a frog but spits it out. Then Minnie is chased by a mink that seems intent on eating her.

A large owl comes and snatches Minnie up. As she flies through the air, Minnie sees Max, stuck in a tree and meowing piteously. When Minnie begs to be let go, she startles the owl who drops her into the tree beside Max.

The two cats set off in the snow looking for home, but are lost. A wildcat leads them back to the mouse hole. Max and Minnie realize they are house cats. They do not belong in the wet, wild woods. The next day, the magic mouse hole is gone.

Discussion Starters and Multidisciplinary Activities

1 This story is a blend of realism and fantasy. Once the students have read the story, ask them to discuss what parts of the story might really happen and what parts are fantasy.

2 Max and Minnie dreamed of hunting in the woods, but when they found themselves there, things were not nearly as nice and pleasant as in their dreams. Ask students if they have ever wished or dreamed of doing something, and then, when they did it, found it disappointing.

3 Max and Minnie chased certain animals in the woods and were chased by others. Ask students what they thought would happen in the story when Max and Minnie met up with a wildcat. Did they expect the wildcat to be helpful? Why or why not?

4 There are many kinds of owls. One kind is pictured in the book. Ask a pair of students to do research to find pictures of owls. Can they identify the owl in the book? Ask them to share with the class what they learn.

5 Cats seem to enjoy sleeping by the fire. Sometimes they twitch as if they are dreaming. Invite students to write a short poem in which they describe a cat's dream. Allow time for those student who wish to share their poems with the class to do so.

6 The author of *Max and Minnie* lives with her two cats in England near the Yorkshire Moors. Ask two students to find out what a moor is and the location of the Yorkshire Moors. Have the students share the information.

📖 *Mrs. Peachtree and the Eighth Avenue Cat*

● **FICTION**

by Erica Silverman
Illustrated by Ellen Beier
New York: Macmillan, 1994. 32p.

This story, illustrated with watercolors, will be enjoyed by primary grade readers.

In New York City at the turn of the century, Mrs. Peachtree runs a tea shop on Eighth Avenue. The first time she sees a stray cat appear in her window, she tries to chase it away, but the cat does not leave. That night, Mrs. Peachtree takes down a bit of chicken for the cat.

The next day the cat comes into the shop with the postman. It jumps up and topples tins of tea, so Mrs. Peachtree chases the cat back outside. But the cat does not leave. Instead, it follows Mrs. Peachtree on her errands, and she continues to feed it.

One day, the cat presents her with a mouse it has caught. Mrs. Peachtree sweeps the mouse and the cat out of her store.

One night when there is a storm, a customer asks Mrs. Peachtree about her cat. Mrs. Peachtree says that she does not own a cat, but the kind old lady begins to worry. It is rainy, windy, and lightning is flashing. Mrs. Peachtree puts on her raincoat and goes out into the storm to search for the cat.

She cannot find it that evening and goes looking again the next morning, but no one has seen the cat. Mrs. Peachtree thinks that the cat is gone, but soon it appears again with the mailman. Mrs. Peachtree decides she does have a cat after all, and names the cat Shadow.

Discussion Starters and Multidisciplinary Activities

1 Mrs. Peachtree is always saying, "Scat, cat!" Ask students if they think Mrs. Peachtree really wanted the cat to stay or go away. Have students list things Mrs. Peachtree did in the story that supports their opinions.

2 Twice when it gets inside the tea shop, the cat knocks things down. But it also catches a mouse. Ask students to discuss whether they think having a cat in a shop would be a bother or a help.

3 Ask students who have read the book what they think will happen next. Will Mrs. Peachtree continue to put out food for the cat, or will she bring the cat into the store and let it stay inside like a pet?

4 Students who read this book will notice that people dress differently from the way people dress today. Ask a pair of students to do research about fashions in the United States around 1900. Have them share the pictures they find with the rest of the class.

5 People deliver things to Mrs. Peachtree's shop in wagons. Students may be surprised that there are no cars or trucks. Invite a pair of students to find out and report to the class when the first car was made in the United States and what it looked like.

6 In this story, an ice man is delivering blocks of ice in a wagon. Ask a pair of students to find out and report when refrigerators came into common use in the United States.

📖 *Out of Nowhere*

FICTION

by Ouida Sebestyen
New York: Orchard Books, 1994. 183p.

Told in the third person from the viewpoint of Harley Nunn, this story describes a young boy on his own after being abandoned by his mother. It will be enjoyed by fourth- and fifth-grade readers.

As the story opens, Harley's mother, Vernie, drives off with her newest boyfriend, leaving Harley behind in a camping area near a lake in Arizona. At the same time some people in a truck abandon a dog. Also in the camping area is a seventy-one-year-old woman, May, who has been abandoned by her husband. May is returning to her childhood home to start a new life. Reluctantly, May gives Harley and the dog, Ish, a ride with her.

When they arrive at May's home they learn that the tenant, Bill, has not moved out. A teenaged girl, Bill's dog, and a pile of junk are waiting for them. They find that Bill recently fell and is recovering in the hospital. He is a great junk collector and the house and nearby shed are jammed full.

May struggles with setting the house in order, painting, and planting a garden. Harley, the girl named Singer, and Bill assist her. Singer teaches love and acceptance by example, but Harley has a difficult time learning, and runs away. Bill goes after Harley, and Ish falls from the truck shattering his leg. Harley helps Bill and May, and earns some money to pay a vet bill. Singer, feeling her work is over, decides to leave. May accepts Harley and Ish into her life and makes room for Bill to stay in the shed.

Discussion Starters and Multidisciplinary Activities

1 Harley, Ish, and May have all been abandoned. Encourage students to discuss the different feelings of hurt and abandonment that each must face.

2 In some ways Singer seems superhuman, almost like a guardian angel that has been dropped into the lives of these people. Have students discuss the ways in which Singer seems "too good to be true." Do the students think that she is a believable character?

3 Singer is away from her father; Harley is away from his mother; May is away from her husband. Bill, it seems, has always been alone and on his own. But Bill must face as many changes and adjustments as anyone else in the story. Encourage students to discuss all the changes Bill is making in his life.

4 Ish is a pit bull. These dogs have had a tremendous amount of bad publicity because of attacks on people. Encourage a pair of students to research newspaper and magazine articles on pit bulls and have them report to the class what they learn.

5 Bill's old car, for which he hopes to get a good price, is a 1931 Model A Ford. Ask a pair of students to research early automobiles. See if they can find a picture of a 1931 Model A to share with the class.

6 Near the end of the book, May brings a new kitten home. With the help of a media specialist, ask a pair of students to find and bring to class a magazine article discussing the importance of pets in the lives of elderly people.

 **A Question of Trust**

by Marion Dane Bauer
New York: Scholastic, 1994. 134p.

F B3255q

FICTION

This story is told in the third person from the viewpoint of Brad, a young boy whose parents have just separated. It will be enjoyed by fourth- and fifth-grade readers, especially boys.

Brad's mother is moving into her own small apartment, leaving behind her two sons, Brad, the oldest, and Charlie who is eight. She calls every Friday and wants the boys to spend weekends with her, but Brad has decided if they never take her calls or go to see her, their mother will become so lonely that she will come home. It is a constant struggle for Brad to keep Charlie from talking to his mother or going to see her.

A stray cat wanders into their back shed and delivers two kittens. Brad connives to claim the black kitten, which he calls Tuxedo, for his own, leaving a tortoise-colored kitten for Charlie. One day they discover Tuxedo dead and half-eaten. Thinking the mother cat killed her kitten, the boys chase her away and take on the responsibility of caring for the other kitten, Muddle. They keep the cats a secret from their worried and distracted father. Brad even takes money from his father's wallet to buy a cat bed and food.

Brad and Charlie fight, and Charlie incorrectly thinks the mother cat has returned to kill Muddle. He sprays water at the cat until it falls from a tree. Charlie runs to his mother's apartment. Brad tells his father the truth and they take both cats to the vet, before Brad also reunites with his mother.

Discussion Starters and Multidisciplinary Activities

1. Ask students to discuss if they think Brad was right in believing that if the two boys told their father about the cat and kittens he would take them to the Humane Society. Or, would he have let the boys keep the kittens? Ask students to use details from the story to support their points of view.

2. The boys had a difficult time naming the kittens. Invite students to suggest what names they would have given these two kittens if they had found them.

3. When the story ends, the two boys have reunited with their mother. Their parents had always wanted to share the boys. Ask students to discuss what they think will happen next? Will both boys live with their father and spend weekends with their mother, or will one or both go to live with their mother?

4. Brad and Charlie go to the library to try to learn more about raising kittens and discover some information about tortoise-colored cats. Ask two students to research this topic. What kinds of cats produce tortoise-colored kittens? What is special or unusual about these kittens?

5. This book has no illustrations. Invite interested students to illustrate a section of the book and to share these illustrations with classmates.

6. On page 92, Brad shakes Charlie hard. We learn about Brad's feelings after this incident, but not about Charlie's. Have students write a page or two describing this incident from Charlie's viewpoint.

📖 *Shiloh* F N234sh

FICTION

by Phyllis Reynolds Naylor
New York: Atheneum, 1991. 144p.

Eleven-year-old Marty, who lives in the country in West Virginia with his parents and two young sisters, tells this story. It will be enjoyed by fourth- and fifth-grade readers.

Marty loves animals but his family has little money and certainly no extra funds to buy or feed pets. When Marty meets a beagle in the woods that follows him home, it is love at first sight. The dog, which Marty named Shiloh, belongs to a neighbor, Judd Travers. Marty is certain that the dog has been mistreated by Judd and he does not want to return it.

Marty's father insists that they return the dog and Marty is miserable. When Shiloh runs away again, Marty decides to keep him in a pen on the hill near his home. Marty's life grows complicated as he lies to sneak food to the dog and keep its presence a secret from his family and friends.

Later, a German shepherd leaps into the pen where Marty is hiding Shiloh and hurts the beagle. The vet takes care of the wounds, but now the family knows about the dog. Marty's father says that as soon as the dog is well it must be returned to Judd.

Marty goes to talk to Judd and sees him shoot a doe. In exchange for keeping quiet about the illegal shooting of the deer and for working twenty hours for Judd, Marty is able to earn his dog, Shiloh. He learns that few things in life are as simple as they seem.

Discussion Starters and Multidisciplinary Activities

1   Although Marty frightens his little sister with snake stories, there are several examples in the book that indicate the brother and his two sisters get along well. Ask students to use examples from the book to describe how the siblings feel about one another.

2   Marty's mother agrees to keep his secret about Shiloh for one night, but her husband learns about it before she tells him. Have students discuss whether they think Marty's mother was right to keep his secret about the dog.

3   There are examples in the last quarter of the book to show that Judd may not be quite as bad as Marty originally thought. What does Judd say or do to support this?

4   Beagles are excellent hunting dogs because of their fine noses. This ability to scent also makes them valuable to law enforcement officials. A beagle brigade is used at some airports to sniff out smuggling activities. Ask a pair of students to research this and report to the class what they learn.

5   In this story, a doctor serves as a veterinarian. Many students are interested in medicine as a career. Have a small group of students research the necessary training to become a doctor or vet and report what they learn.

6   This book won a Newbery Medal. Ask a pair of students to research more about this medal. In what year was it first presented? Which book won the medal last year? Have them report what they learn.

From *Exploring the World of Animals.* © 1997. Teacher Ideas Press. (800) 237-6124.

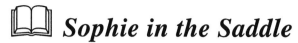 *Sophie in the Saddle*

FICTION

by Dick King-Smith
Illustrated by David Parkins
Cambridge, MA: Candlewick Press, 1994. 92p.

This book will be enjoyed by readers in second and third grade. It was first printed in Great Britain in 1993 and is the fourth book in a series about Sophie, the others being *Sophie's Snail*, *Sophie's Tom*, and *Sophie Hits Six*.

Sophie is a very determined little girl who lives in England and whose birthday falls on Christmas Day. She has two older brothers, Matthew and Mark. More than anything else, Sophie wants to be a lady farmer. She loves animals and already has a black cat called Tomboy and a white rabbit named Beano. The family gets a puppy for Christmas, and Sophie names the little terrier Puddles.

Sophie's Aunt Al, who lives in the Highlands and is nearly eighty-two years old, telephones to tell Sophie that she is responsible for housebreaking and training the puppy. Sophie takes her job seriously, and the puppy becomes reasonably well-behaved.

Sophie learns to swim and, as a reward for her efforts, she is allowed to take Puddles with them on the family's two-week summer vacation. They go to stay at a farm that is close to the beach in Cornwall. Each sunny day the family goes to the beach and swims. Each day Sophie also has a riding lesson. The farmer's wife teaches Sophie to ride on a horse named Bumblebee.

Sophie has many adventures on the farm and at the beach before she and her family return home with Puddles.

Discussion Starters and Multidisciplinary Activities

1 As students read this story they will quickly notice that Sophie often confuses one word for another, such as amateur for immature and persecuted for prosecuted. Ask students to keep track of these words and to write simple definitions for them.

2 Sophie and her brothers tease each other but get along reasonably well. With a small group of students who have read the book, discuss some of the events that show that Sophie's brothers are proud of her and try to be helpful.

3 Because this book was first published in England, it contains many expressions not familiar to Americans. With a small group of students, discuss some of the expressions in the book that sound English and describe how an American author might have expressed these same ideas differently.

4 Sophie explains that in her piggy bank she had saved ten pounds and ten pence toward buying her farm. Ask a pair of students to research and report how much that is in American currency.

5 Sophie and her family vacation in Cornwall. Invite a pair of interested students to find out where Cornwall is located and what cities in Cornwall are famous as vacation areas. These students should share what they learn.

6 Jo has a pet Vietnamese potbellied pig. These pigs have recently become very popular as pets. Ask a group of students to find more information about these pigs and report back what they learn.

 *Windsong*

by Lynn Hall
New York: Charles Scribner's Sons, 1992. 73p.

FICTION

This book deals with problems in a family and a girl's need for attention. She seeks love by trying to raise a greyhound puppy named Windsong. It will be enjoyed by fourth- and fifth-grade readers. A thirteen-year-old girl named Marty tells this story.

Marty lives with her mother, father, and brother, Matt, in a small town in Missouri. Marty is convinced that her parents, particularly her father, love Matt more than her. Matt has a number of allergies and uses this to get his way.

Marty spends as much time as possible with Orland, who has a kennel and races greyhounds. Orland gives Marty a pup that she takes home and keeps in a fort in the backyard. Her mother agrees with Marty that it will be all right to keep the dog outside. Matt, however, sneaks into the fort and comes inside wheezing from his allergies, so the dog, Windsong, must go.

Marty gives the dog to her music teacher. The music teacher, Ushie, soon grows attached to the dog and is irritated with Marty when she comes over early in the morning and wants to take the dog away with her for the day.

Marty discovers her mother hugging and kissing Brother George, a charismatic preacher. Marty also discovers her father crying. Marty wrestles with whether to help break up her family in hopes that she will live with her mother and be able to get Windsong back, or whether she should help keep her family together.

Discussion Starters and Multidisciplinary Activities

1 Some people in the book suggest that Marty is selfish. Allow students to discuss this. Is it selfish to want to feel loved? Is it selfish to want a pet? Is Marty less selfish at the end of the book than she was at the beginning?

2 Marty's music teacher is a strange character. She no longer teaches Marty but continues to take money for music lessons. She seems friendly and willing to help out with Windsong at the beginning, but then is difficult when Marty wants to spend time with the dog. Let students discuss the character, Ushie, and share how they feel about her.

3 Right now Marty wants to race greyhounds. She is absolutely certain about this, but many people change their plans about the future as they grow up. Allow students to discuss if they think Marty will still want to be a dog racer in five years. Why do they feel as they do?

4 Greyhound racing, like horse racing, involves betting. In some states dog racing is a popular sport. Invite a pair of students to research greyhound racing and report what they learn.

5 Ask a pair of students to predict if dogs or cats are the more popular pet in their class. Then have students poll the class to find out.

6 Other than the cover, this book has no pictures. Invite interested students to use any medium to create an illustration for the book. Share these pictures.

◆ *Bridges and Poetry* ◆

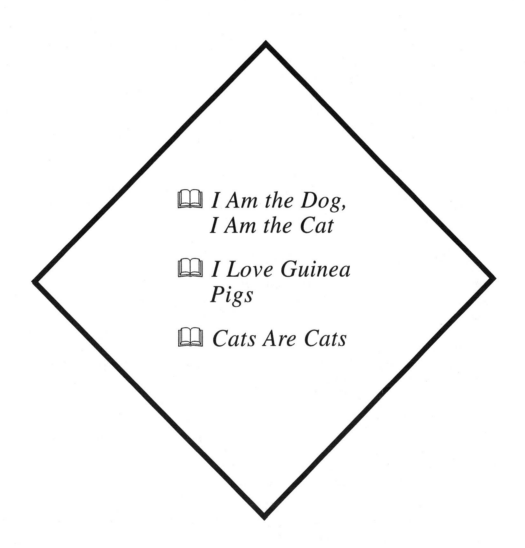

  📖 *I Am the Dog,*
   I Am the Cat

  📖 *I Love Guinea*
   Pigs

  📖 *Cats Are Cats*

📖 *I Am the Dog, I Am the Cat*

by Donald Hall
Illustrated by Barry Moser   *F H 141i*
New York: Dial Books, 1994. 32p.

This large-format picture book will appeal to primary-grade students. Full-page illustrations are colorful and realistic. The biography format of a dog and a cat works as a "bridge" between fiction and nonfiction.

First the dog, and later the cat, give their impressions about eating. The dog admits to liking bones and especially to having its owners feed it. The cat sometimes teases to be fed and then turns up its nose at what is offered.

The dog lets visiting babies pull its hair, while the cat tries to vanish when babies appear. The dog barks and protects the house from burglars and kidnappers, while the cat welcomes strangers if it feels like sitting on a comfortable lap.

Both animals admit to sleeping a lot, but the cat insists that it works hard and keeps awake at night on mouse patrol, or at least in hunting paper and rubber bands. The dog likes to chase rabbits and roll in anything that smells good. The cat paws at a door and then refuses to go through it, or acts frightened and runs and hides.

The dog admits to being frightened of loud noises, but the cat insists that nothing really frightens it. The dog is "the nose," and always sniffs at things, while the cat watches birds from the window. The cat is amused that the dog cares what people think of it. Each thinks that the other is weird.

Possible Topics for Further Investigation

1. Among students there will undoubtedly be both "dog lovers" and "cat lovers." Some students, of course, will adore both. All are likely to be entranced by the presentation of the opposite dog and cat viewpoints presented throughout this book. Using this story as a model, suggest that students write an original short book in which they portray "opposites." Topics might be a messy and a neat child, the world view of a mouse and an elephant, a baby using "baby talk" with an adult using "grown-up talk," etc. Students might illustrate their stories with pictures. Allow time for sharing.

2. Invite someone from the Humane Society to come to the classroom and talk about the Society and the importance of the proper care of pets and animals. As a follow-up activity, include pet care posters made by students with a thank-you letter to the guest speaker. The posters should contain short slogans indicating what the students learned from their guest speaker.

3. There are always news items that feature the adventures of dogs and cats. Sometimes there are stories about animals that travel great distances to get back to their original homes. Other times, a dog wakes a family and saves people from a fire. Search and rescue dogs or guide dogs may make the news, or a cat may be rescued from a tree top. Invite students to look for dog and cat stories that appear in newspapers or magazines. Ask the students to photocopy or clip these stories and post them on a class bulletin board.

I Love Guinea Pigs

by Dick King-Smith
Illustrated by Anita Jeram
Cambridge, MA: Candlewick Press, 1994. 28p.

◆
**BRIDGES
AND POETRY**

This bridge book combines elements of fiction (exciting story and good illustrations) with elements of nonfiction (interesting facts and ideas). It will be enjoyed by readers in the primary grades.

The book begins by explaining that guinea pigs are not pigs, but are rodents like mice, rats, and squirrels. Like other rodents, a guinea pig has special front teeth that are good for gnawing things and that grow throughout the animal's life. Guinea pigs were brought to Europe about four hundred years ago from Dutch Guiana. Their name gradually changed to guinea pigs.

Guinea pigs come in many different colors and can be smooth-coated, rough-coated, and long-coated. The author explains that he has had hundreds of guinea pigs and likes the Abyssinians best. Guinea pigs need a roomy hutch or wire pen in the yard in a place where they can be warm and dry. Properly cared for, pet guinea pigs usually live from five to eight years.

Guinea pig food is available in pellets, but the animals also like cabbage and cauliflower leaves, carrots, bread, apple peelings, dandelions, and clover, as well as clean drinking water every day. They whistle and make a variety of sounds.

Guinea pigs become fond of people who handle them regularly and stroke and talk to them. Baby guinea pigs are born full-furred with eyes open.

Possible Topics for Further Investigation

1   Guinea pigs are often kept as pets both at home and in the classroom because they are easy to care for and enjoy being held and petted. Try to find someone in your school who keeps a pet guinea pig and invite that person to visit the classroom and bring the guinea pig along. The guest can tell about the pet, including what it eats, how old it is, and what kind of guinea pig it is. After the visit, have students write a letter to the guest thanking him or her for coming and share something that the students learned as a result of the visit.

2   A few students who may be especially interested in guinea pigs might do further research with the help of the school media specialist, and share what they learn. They might find pictures they could clip or photocopy to put on a bulletin board, or draw pictures of their own to post along with information such as the names of the different types of guinea pigs and any interesting facts.

3   This book mentions that guinea pigs were introduced to Europe from a country in South America called Dutch Guiana. Guinea pigs are members of the cavy family and their scientific names are *Cavia procellus*. Invite a small group of students to research the cavy family. Have them locate Dutch Guiana on a map. What other animals are in the cavy family in addition to guinea pigs? Do the other family members live in the wild or are they kept as pets? Where do these animals live? Do they have any commercial uses?

 *Cats Are Cats* 808.1

L328c

compiled by Nancy Larrick
Drawings by Ed Young
New York: Philomel Books, 1988. 80p.

◆
**BRIDGES
AND POETRY**

This is a collection of forty-two poems written by many different poets on the topic of cats. The book contains an index of poets, of poems, and of first lines.

There is a short introduction to this book by the compiler, Nancy Larrick, in which she notes that people who have grown to know and love cats realize that in any house where a cat lives, it is the cat that makes the decisions.

The poems include discussions of mysterious cats, the habits of cats, snarling cats who fight in alleys, curious cats, and proud cats. Each reader will find a favorite.

Several of the poems try to describe the mystery of a cat in moonlight or against the snow. Among these are: The Open Door and On a Night of Snow, by Elizabeth Coatsworth; Cat in Moonlight, by Douglas Gibson; Cat at Night, by Adrien Stoutenburg; and That Cat, by Karla Kuskin.

Other poems take a more humorous look at cats, such as: My Cat, Mrs. Lick-a-Chin, by John Ciardi; This Cat, Rosalie the Cat, and Pictures of Cats, by Karla Kuskin; Our Cat, by Marchette Chute; Cat, by John Aiken; Chang McTang McQuarter Cat, by John Ciardi; The Mysterious Cat, by Vachel Lindsay; Cat Cat, by Eve Merriam; A Different Door, by X. J. Kennedy; Cats Sleep Fat, by Rosalie Moore; and Cat, by William J. Smith.

Discussion Starters and Multidisciplinary Activities

1 Choose a group of poems that discuss the ways cats behave and read these to the class. Included might be "Kitten," by Valerie Worth; "Confidence," by Martha Baird; and "Apartment Cats," by Thom Gunn. Then allow time for students to describe the behavior of cats they have known.

2 Read two poems, one that describes the mystery of cats and one that describes an alley cat. Choices might be "Cat in Moonlight," by Douglas Gibson and "The Tomcat," by Don Marquis. Encourage students to study how particular words are used by poets to achieve quite different impressions of cats.

3 John Ciardi's poem, "The Cat Heard the Cat-Bird," is filled with all kinds of rhyme. Take time to study the internal and end rhymes with students. Discuss the effect of having so much rhyme in one poem.

4 Cats are often associated with Halloween. Read Shelagh McGee's poem, "Wanted—A Witch's Cat," orally. Then encourage students to write their own newspaper ad for a witch's cat. Take time to share these.

5 Some poems lend themselves well to choral reading, using solo voices, and groups of high and low voices. Take Vachel Lindsay's poem, "The Mysterious Cat," and, with the students, prepare it as a choral reading to share with another class.

6 Share William Jay Smith's "Cat" poem, which tells how cats differ from people. Ask the students to add another stanza. Share the results.

From *Exploring the World of Animals*. © 1997. Teacher Ideas Press. (800) 237-6124.

Nonfiction Connections

📖 *Gerbils*

📖 *Hedgehogs: How to Take Care of Them and Understand Them*

📖 *Helping Our Animal Friends*

📖 *How to Look After Your Rabbit*

📖 *Kitten Care and Critters, Too!*

📖 *Patrol Dogs: Keeping the Peace*

📖 *The Pets You Love*

📖 *A Puppy Is Born*

📖 *Rosie, A Visiting Dog's Story*

📖 *Taking Care of Your Dog*

📖 *Why Mammals Have Fur*

 *Gerbils*

by Norman Barrett
New York: Franklin Watts, 1990. 32p.

This book is about half text and half color photographic illustrations. It is part of a Picture Library series of visual reference books. It will be enjoyed by readers in second through fifth grade.

The book begins by explaining that gerbils are small, furry animals that make good pets because they are gentle and easy to care for. Gerbils squeak only when frightened. They are members of the rodent family and are closely related to hamsters and muskrats. Like most rodents, they have incisors that continue to grow throughout life and that are worn away by gnawing. Gerbils have a body about 4 inches long and a tail of equal length. They have strong claws that are used for digging.

In the wild, gerbils dig burrows in which they remain during the day, coming out at night to hunt for seeds, leaves, and roots. They often live in family groups with several burrows, six or seven entrances, and a main tunnel. Their enemies are foxes, snakes, and owls.

In the section on birth and growing up, the text explains that gerbils can have from one to twelve young, with an average of four or five. The newborns are blind, deaf, toothless, and without fur. By twelve weeks, the babies are full grown.

Mongolian gerbils are most common as pets. Other species include pygmy gerbils, short-tailed or bushy-tailed gerbils, and hairy-footed gerbils.

Possible Topics for Further Investigation

1   The text explains that there are about eighty species of wild gerbils, most of which live in the dry regions of Africa and Asia. Have a small group of students, with the help of a media specialist, research more about gerbils in the wild. What are some of these species? How do they differ from one another? Do they have any commercial uses? Are they regarded as pests? What do they eat in the wild, and in turn, what preys upon them? When students have collected information they should make an oral report to the class on gerbils in the wild.

2   A French missionary, Pere David, is credited with being the first European to discover gerbils. He wrote about them in 1866 and sent specimens from China to the Paris Museum of Natural History. With the help of a media specialist, ask a pair of students to find out more about Pere David. How long was he in China? Did he return to France? Why was he interested in gerbils? Findings should be shared with the class.

3   Gerbils are among the animals often used for laboratory research. Ask a small group of students to read magazine articles dealing with laboratory research animals. Why do some people feel animals should not be used for these purposes, while others feel such research is essential? Ask students to present a panel discussion during which they discuss considerations involved in choosing to use or not to use animals for laboratory research.

📖 *Hedgehogs: How to Take Care of Them and Understand Them*

NONFICTION CONNECTIONS

by Matthew M. Vriends

Hauppauge, NY: Barron's Educational Series, 1995. 88p.

This book is written as a manual. It has small print and is illustrated with color photos and line drawings. It will be enjoyed by third- through fifth-grade readers.

The author explains that hedgehogs are not native to North America, but recently have become popular pets. The African pygmy hedgehog is about 6 inches long from snout to tail, weighs one pound, and makes a good pet for people with limited space. The hedgehog is usually docile and quite intelligent.

Hedgehogs are mammals known as insectivores. Most insectivores have five toes on each foot, a sharply pointed snout, and small eyes. They are found throughout the world, from Australia and New Zealand, to Asia, Europe, and Africa. They feed mainly on insects but also eat slugs, snails, spiders, nestling birds, small rodents, and reptiles. Hedgehogs are active at night and consume almost their own weight in food nightly. In winter, European hedgehogs hibernate and live on energy from stored fat. In other parts of the world, some hedgehogs go into aestivation (summer sleep) during the dry season.

The back and sides of hedgehogs are covered in barbless spines. The face, limbs, tail, and stomach have hair. They have large incisors and 36 to 44 teeth.

Hedgehogs can become excellent household pets, living for eight to ten years. They are neat, clean, and affectionate. Their cages must be kept clean and food pellets supplemented.

Possible Topics for Further Investigation

1. Two well-known pieces of children's literature contain hedgehogs. Mrs. Tiggy-Wiggle is the hedgehog written about by Beatrix Potter, and hedgehogs were used as croquet balls in Lewis Carroll's *Alice in Wonderland*. Invite two groups of students to study these selections, and then present a dramatic scene involving the hedgehogs. They may include dialogue and use simple costumes and props in presenting their short plays.

2. This book contains the names and addresses of two sources of newsletters about hedgehogs: North American Hedgehog Association, 601 Tijeras Avenue NW, Suite 201, Albuquerque, NM 87102 and *Exotic Market Review*, P.O. Box 1203, Bowie, TX 76230. Students who are interested in hedgehogs as pets might write to these two addresses requesting a back issue of their newsletter. A stamped and self-addressed envelope should be included for reply. Responses might be shared with other interested class members.

3. There is a warning in this book that when people who are handling pets, such as hedgehogs, are scratched or bitten, there is a danger of tetanus infection. This disease is caused by a bacillus, *Clostridium tetani*, which enters the body through the wound. People also get this infection by being cut by a nail or piece of metal on which a bacillus lives. Invite a doctor to explain more about tetanus, how it affects human beings, and the purpose of periodic shots to minimize the danger from tetanus. Follow up with a thank-you letter.

📖 *Helping Our Animal Friends*

by Judith E. Rinard
Washington, DC: National Geographic Society, 1985. 34p.

This book is one of a series called Books for Young Explorers. It has a large format, simple text, and is illustrated with full-color photographs. The book will be enjoyed by second- through fourth-grade readers.

The book begins with a vet giving a dog a thorough examination. Seeing that a pet gets regular checkups is one of the many things that a responsible pet owner does. Pet owners can supply a box for a cat and her kittens, make sure that ducks have water in which to swim and preen their feathers, and supply proper amounts of food and water. Pet owners need to assure that some pets, like big dogs, get outdoor exercise every day.

During the snowy months, many animals that live outdoors need help from people. Some people put seeds in bird feeders. Farmers put out hay for their cows and calves. Animals that live indoors need to have their tanks or cages cleaned regularly.

Many animals such as horses and dogs need baths and may also need brushing, and sheep need sheering. Horses must have their hooves polished. Animals who are orphaned, abandoned, sick, or injured may need special help from park rangers or from an animal shelter.

Animals also need love and attention. Teaching them to be well behaved not only makes it pleasant to have them around, but it also may prevent pets from getting into dangerous situations and being hurt.

Possible Topics for Further Investigation

1   An interested student may want to build a squirrel feeder to place on a window sill. To build a feeder, cut two pieces of wood 20 inches long and 10 inches wide. These are the top and bottom of the feeder. The sides should be 10 inches square. Screw the top and bottom to the sides and attach the feeder to a windowsill. Also screw a piece of wood to the floor of the feeder to one side. This post should be about 4 inches tall with a base that's about 1 inch square. You can put peanuts, dried corn, or bits of apple in the feeder. In winter you might tie a pinecone to the post and push pieces of fruit or raisins among the bracts of the cone.

2   Some students might want to make a toy for a cat. Cut two circles from a piece of material. Place wrong sides together and sew the circles together, leaving a small hole about an inch wide. Turn the fabric right side out. Stuff the circle of cloth with dried catnip. Sew up the small hole you left. You might also want to attach a string with a bell. Cats will enjoy chewing, batting, and pouncing on the toy.

3   For a class project, make a set of pet safety posters. With permission, these posters might be hung for a week throughout the halls of the school. Each poster should have a drawing or design as well as a short slogan. Examples include: Don't Lock Dogs in Hot Cars. Be Sure Your Pet Has Fresh Water. Have You Hugged Your Dog Today? Support the Local Humane Society. Does Your Pet Need to See a Vet?

📖 *How to Look After Your Rabbit*

■ **NONFICTION CONNECTIONS**

by Colin Hawkins and Jacqui Hawkins
Cambridge, MA: Candlewick Press, 1995. 28p.

This book has a simple text and is illustrated with comical and colorful drawings. It is one of a series of books on how to care for small pets and will be enjoyed by second- through fourth-grade readers.

The book begins with rabbit history and traces rabbits from the time they lived in northern Europe and were forced to move south during the Ice Age. This Common European rabbit, which is native to Spain, is the ancestor of the domestic breeds.

There is a section on choosing a rabbit for a pet. They make good pets because they are clean and gentle and should live about five years. Smaller breeds are easier to hold when fully grown. It is best to buy a rabbit in spring when it is nine to twelve weeks old. A female rabbit is called a doe and a male rabbit is called a buck. Because rabbits are sociable, you may wish to choose two does from the same litter for pets.

A large rabbit hutch in a shed makes a good home. If the hutch is placed outdoors it needs to be sheltered from cold, wind, and sun. The hutch should contain a separate sleeping area that is lined with absorbent material.

Rabbits need a heavy food dish that will not tip over and a drip-fed water bottle. Giving a rabbit a piece of wood to gnaw will help stop its teeth from growing too long. Rabbits will eat pellets and enjoy fresh greens, carrots, and fruits. Hay is also an important part of a rabbit's diet.

Possible Topics for Further Investigation

1. The illustrations used in this book are colorful and cartoonlike with bubbles containing words to indicate dialogue. If a student in the class is a budding cartoonist, encourage him or her to do a single cartoon or an ongoing comic strip featuring one of the rabbits shown in this book. Both pictures and a caption or dialogue can be used. The rabbit can get in and out of amusing predicaments. The cartoon or comic strip might be posted on the class bulletin board.

2. A group of students might pair up to provide material for a class bulletin board. Each pair of students will research one breed of rabbits. One will write a report about the rabbit, while the other will supply an illustration. Illustrations may be original drawings, photocopies, or clippings from magazines. Among the rabbits to be researched, students might choose lop-eared, Dutch, English, Spotted English, angora, mini rex, orange rex, rex, Belgian hare, Netherland dwarf, or Flemish giant.

3. Many humorous poems have been written about animals. "The Hippopotamus" by Jack Prelutsky, "Three Hens" by Henry Johnstone, "Ant and Eleph-Ant" by Spike Milligan, "Yak" by William Jay Smith, and "The Whale" by Theodore Roethke are among these. Read orally some humorous poems about animals and then invite class members to write original "funny bunny" poems. These humorous poems about rabbits can be shared on a class bulletin board, or they might be typed and reproduced as a class book of poetry.

636.8
P442K

📖📖 *Kitten Care and Critters, Too!*

**NONFICTION
CONNECTIONS**

by Judy Petersen-Fleming and Bill Fleming
New York: Tambourine Books, 1994. 40p.

This book shows children the basic steps in caring for animals by stressing similarities between young house pets and animals that live in zoos and wildlife parks. It is a large-format book with simple text and contains many color photographs. It will be enjoyed by primary-grade readers.

The book begins by showing how the care of a kitten at home is similar to the care of tiger cubs with their trainer. The authors emphasize the proper way to lift and support a kitten.

They explain that a kitten may feel frightened when it first comes home. The pet owner needs to spend time with the kitten and, if possible, place it in a quiet room with a soft bed. This helps the kitten feel calm and secure. On the facing page the reader learns that a baby orangutan also likes a soft blanket and being petted by its trainer when it is small. This format of contrasting a kitten page with a facing critter page is used throughout the book.

During the first three months of a kitten's life it is important for the pet owner to spend a lot of time with the kitten. This is compared to the amount of time a trainer must give a baby penguin so that it feels secure and happy.

The book continues to contrast the care of a kitten with the care of a koala bear, gazelle, wallaby, lion, tiger, giraffe, chimpanzee, swan, polar bear, and a manatee.

Possible Topics for Further Investigation

1   This book provides addresses of four special parks and zoos where students might visit animals. Ask a pair of students to write to these four places, including a stamped, self-addressed envelope, and requesting pamphlets. The materials received should be shared with the class. The addresses are Marine World Africa U.S.A., Marine World Parkway, Vallejo, CA 94589; San Diego Zoo, 2920 Zoo Drive, San Diego, CA 92109; Sea World of Florida, 7007 Sea World Drive, Orlando, FL 32821; and Sea World of California, 1720 South Shores Road, San Diego, CA 92109.

2   Page 9 of this book shows a sea otter and informs us that the fur of a sea otter has more hairs per square inch than any other animal in the world. Invite a pair of students to research sea otters. Where do they live? What kinds of food do they eat? What are their chief enemies? Why is their fur so thick? Is the fur used for any commercial purpose? Have the students prepare a short written report with a bibliography that indicates the sources of their information.

3   A koala bear is pictured on page 15. The text explains that koala means "bear with a leather bag." In spite of the name, koala bears are not really related to bears. They are somewhat similar to kangaroos in that they carry their young in a pouch. Ask a small group of students to research koala bears. Where do they live? What do they eat? What are their enemies? How do they care for their young? How large do they grow? Ask the students to give an oral report to the class.

 *Patrol Dogs: Keeping the Peace*

by Elizabeth Ring
Brookfield, CT: Millbrook Press, 1994. 32p.

NONFICTION CONNECTIONS

This book is part of a series of books, Good Dogs!, which describe the kinds of dogs that play important roles in our lives. It is illustrated with black-and-white and color photos and will be enjoyed by readers in third through fifth grades.

The book begins by telling the story of Rondo, a German shepherd police dog, who won Colorado's Medal of Valor for his bravery in disarming a woman who was waving a pistol and frightening everyone. Rondo was wounded in the attack, but was soon back on the job. Rondo is one of many dogs trained to be a partner to a police officer. These teams patrol an area, either on foot or in a car.

The reader learns that New York City began using dogs in police work in 1907. By the 1950s K-9 corps were in use in hundreds of towns and cities throughout the United States. German shepherds are considered the best all-around police dogs, but other breeds are also used. Labrador retrievers and golden retrievers, often called D-dogs, are trained to sniff out narcotics and bombs. Bloodhounds are used as trackers.

This book explains the special training that dogs and their partners undergo during three months of learning to work together. Dogs learn to respond to voice and hand signals, and most service dogs live at home with their partners.

Possible Topics for Further Investigation

1. Drill with multiplication and division facts can be made more fun by designing and playing board games. Ask a small group of students to design a math fact board game in which the path around the board is designed to be the trail of a criminal. The playing pieces can be small plastic dogs. On a roll of the die, a player may advance forward the number shown only after correctly answering the top three cards in a pile of fact cards. Special squares might be labeled "lost scent, return to start," or "false trail, retreat 3 squares."

2. Some police departments with K-9 units have teams that visit classrooms and explain their work. Check with your local police department. If an officer and dog are available for a class visit, make arrangements. Help students plan the questions they want to ask ahead of time. Be sure that class members follow up the visit with a thank-you letter.

3. Although police dogs undergo rigorous training, dog obedience classes are frequently offered and prove to be helpful to ordinary household pets. If there is a dog trainer in your community who teaches obedience classes, invite that person to come to school as a guest speaker. If possible, have the trainer bring a dog. Arrange for a place and time outside where the trainer can demonstrate how a pet can be taught to sit, heel, and follow instructions. Ask a pair of students to follow up the visit with a written thank-you letter.

 *The Pets You Love*

by Jennifer C. Urquhart
Washington, DC: National Geographic Society, 1991. 34p.

NONFICTION CONNECTIONS

This book is one in a series published by the National Geographic Society, Books for Young Explorers. It is a large-format book and is illustrated with color photographs. The simple text will be enjoyed by first- through third-grade readers.

The book discusses pets and suggests why one kind may be more appropriate than another. For instance, a child who lives in the city and has a dog will need to have the dog on a leash when on the street so the dog will not run in front of a car. On a farm an unleashed dog will have plenty of running space.

A small pet, such as a parakeet or a gerbil, will spend a lot of time in a cage, which needs to be kept clean. Such pets need food and fresh water. These pets will need to spend some time out of their cages, too. Fish also require care. They need a clean tank, the right amount of food, and plants to help make a good home.

Some pets, like dogs that live in the home, have special needs such as grooming, bathing, housebreaking, and training. Dogs and cats also need to visit a veterinarian for checkups and shots to help keep the animals well.

The conclusion explains that if pets are raised together when they are young, and get to know and like each other, they can often become friends and live together happily.

Possible Topics for Further Investigation

1. The subject of pets presents an opportunity for teaching or reinforcing graphing skills. (For students who do not currently have a pet, ask them to think of a pet they once owned or would like to have when they respond to the graphing tasks.) Using the chalkboard, list the names of kinds of pets along the bottom axis (dogs, cats, birds, fish, etc.). On the vertical axis, list the numerals 0, 1, 2, 3, 4, 5, 6, etc. Each student can fill in a section of a column to represent his or her pet. The graph can then be used for other math questions, such as, which pet is most popular in our class? Are two pets equal in popularity?

2. You may wish to set up a classroom aquarium. If you and your students are experienced in fish care and already have the tank, you may choose to set it up on your own. You can also ask a local fish shop owner to come to school and help you set one up. This expert could discuss the needs of the fish—water temperature, size of tank, plants, and so on, and an appropriate schedule for feeding.

3. Most students like to write about animals. Ask each student to write a short story using an animal in the plot. It could be something that really happened, something that might happen, or a fanciful tale that could never happen. After the stories are complete, set aside a time when those who wish to can share their stories orally.

A Puppy Is Born

by Heiderose Fischer-Nagel and Andreas Fischer-Nagel
New York: G. P. Putnam's Sons, 1985. 38p.

This brief and simple text is illustrated with color photographs. It will be enjoyed by second- through fourth-grade readers.

Max and Missy, wirehaired dachshunds, are featured in this book. As the book opens, Missy is expecting a litter of puppies in two months. In the weeks that follow, Missy eats more than usual and her stomach looks rounder.

When the puppies are ready to be born, Missy goes into her familiar basket. The book describes how she helps by pressing the first puppy out of the opening of her birth canal, which is just under her tail. The newborn is enclosed in a fluid-filled birth sac. Missy breaks open this sac when the puppy is out. During the next hour, Missy has three more puppies. After they are licked clean, they begin to suck warm milk. Each puppy weighs about one-half pound.

The puppies, which cannot see, hear, or smell, spend their first few days sleeping and eating. They snuggle close together for warmth. In a few weeks they can see and begin to sniff and explore. After one month, they begin to explore outside and learn to eat from a bowl. The puppies also chew on everything they can find. Already they have developed distinct personalities, with Charlie being the leader.

In two months the puppies are ready to go to the veterinarian for shots and will go to live with new owners.

Possible Topics for Further Investigation

1. In the beginning of this book, the author explains that certain dogs are considered special because they are pedigreed. Pedigreed means that the dogs are registered in a book that gives their history. The American Kennel Club (AKC) is a group that registers dogs. Ask a pair of students to discover more about registering a dog. What does an application form look like? What fees are involved? Are there special privileges or responsibilities? Students should report what they learn.

2. There are three kinds of dachshunds. Max and Minnie are both wirehaired dachshunds. The other two are longhaired and shorthaired dachshunds. Ask a pair of students to research these three kinds of dachshunds, orally report what they learn, and share a picture of each dachshund while pointing out differences and similarities.

3. The four puppies in this story already have distinct personalities. Charlie is the leader. His brother spends a lot of time in play. Cocoa, a female, is timid and shy, while her sister is lively and playful. Interested students might want to write an adventure story about the puppies before they leave for new homes. They will need to name the other two dogs. This could be a short story or a picture book with illustrations. Allow time for students to share their stories and to explain how they chose to name the other two puppies as they did.

📖 *Rosie, A Visiting Dog's Story*

by Stephanie Calmenson
New York: Clarion Books, 1994. 48p.

This large-format book is illustrated with color photographs. It will be enjoyed by students in all elementary grades.

Rosie, the dog in this story, is a Tibetan terrier. Rosie is an ordinary, friendly puppy who gets into the usual mischief. But as an adult dog, Rosie is special. She is a working dog. Rosie's uniform is a red harness and a special badge that says, "I am a visiting dog." Rosie has to be trained to be a visiting dog. She joins a visiting dog program at the ASPCA when she is two years old.

Rosie must learn to be comfortable around equipment, because some of the people she visits use walkers or wheelchairs or have hospital tubes connected to them. She has to be gentle with children who might pull her hair or tail, or with adults who might pet her roughly. She has to be a good traveler on a train, bus, or airplane.

After four months of training, Rosie is tested. She passes all of her tests and is given her badges. Then Rosie is asked to visit in a children's hospital. Rosie fetches a ball for a girl in a wheelchair, is brushed by a blind boy, and takes a nap beside a boy who is not feeling well.

Rosie makes many other trips. One is to the Village Nursing Home where many sick and lonely older people enjoy petting and talking to Rosie.

Possible Topics for Further Investigation

1 A small group of students might want to find out more about nearby visiting dog programs and the requirements for participation. Students might contact a local animal shelter, a 4-H club, Therapy Dogs International, or a training and educational resource center called The Delta Society® at P.O. Box 1080, Renton, WA 98057-9906. When writing for information, students should enclose a stamped, self-addressed envelope and share any information they might receive with classmates.

2 Rosie needed to have a special pass to travel. People who use trained dogs, such as Seeing Eye dogs, also need to have passes so these dogs can accompany them on public transportation and into buildings where dogs are not usually allowed. Invite a pair of students to learn more about special passes for dogs. Who can request these special passes? Are they free? What agency distributes these passes? The students should share information.

3 If someone in your community uses a Seeing Eye dog and is comfortable visiting the class and discussing the use of the dog, invite that person to come to school. (Special transportation might need to be arranged.) Help the students prepare questions ahead of time. Possible questions include the following: How long have you had the dog? How old is the dog? Did you have special training with this dog? Be sure to follow up the visit with a thank-you letter.

📖 *Taking Care of Your Dog*

by Joyce Pope
New York: Franklin Watts, 1986. 32p.

NONFICTION CONNECTIONS

This book is one in a series with information about choosing, housing, and feeding pets. It is illustrated with color photographs and will be enjoyed by second-through fourth-grade readers.

The author begins by noting that by caring for pets we can find out about other creatures that share our world. It is most important to remember that pets are not toys; they are living creatures that require care and attention.

There are more kinds of dogs than any other domestic animal. Most of these breeds can be trained to be good pets. Since a dog may live for fifteen years, taking in a puppy as a pet means a long-term commitment. Dogs are also expensive to feed and need enough space for outdoor exercise.

The author recommends finding out about as many dog breeds as possible and considering your home environment before choosing. Small dogs, such a Chihuahuas, could live in an apartment. Dogs like Afghan hounds require a lot of time for grooming. Large dogs that grow over 100 pounds like the Great Pyrenees might be hard for a child to control.

Once you have selected a dog, you need to plan for things such as a bed, collar and leash, dog doors, brush, and food and water dishes. Other issues include inoculations, house training, giving the dog a name, praising and feeding it, exercise, play, and obedience.

Possible Topics for Further Investigation

1. In most places, dogs need to have a license. Ask a pair of students to learn more about dog licensing. Where do you go in your town or city to get a dog license? Do you need a new one every year? What information is required? What is the cost? What do you do if your dog loses its license? If your dog runs away or is lost, how is its license useful?

2. A group of students might want to prepare a "Did you know . . .?" bulletin board about dogs. They could clip magazine pictures of dogs or photocopy pictures of various kinds of dogs and post these. They could also include interesting facts. Some facts are given on page 31 of this book. How big is the largest dog? Which is the smallest? How long does an average dog live? How fast can a dog run? What is the scientific name of the dog?

3. Almost everyone has a favorite dog book. To encourage others to read these stories, you might prepare a tempting book of advertisements. Each student would write a brief sales pitch about why classmates might want to read a favorite dog book. The title and author should be included. Some students might want to tempt the reader by telling an exciting part of the story. Others might pose questions which can be answered after reading the book. Put these ads in a three-ring notebook and make it available to students looking for books to read.

📖 *Why Mammals Have Fur*

NONFICTION
CONNECTIONS

by Dorothy Hinshaw Patent
New York: Cobblehill Books, 1995. 26p.

This simple text is illustrated with color photographs. It will be enjoyed by third- through fifth-grade readers.

The book is divided into four chapters, "Animals with Fur," "Living with Fur," "Their Beautiful Coats," and "People and Fur." There is also an index. The author first points out that one reason mammals can live in so many different parts of the world is because of their furry coverings. Without a protective covering, warm-blooded animals would not survive.

No one is sure how fur originated. Each hair grows from a tiny pocket in the skin called a follicle. Experts can tell what kind of animal a hair comes from by studying the scale pattern of the hair. Many animals have guard hairs which are long and straight, and underneath have a dense layer of underfur. Animals may also have special hairs such as eyelashes and whiskers. The quills of a porcupine and the horns of a rhinoceros are also made of compressed hairs.

The book discusses the drawbacks as well as advantages of fur. When fur gets wet it loses its insulating ability. Otters have especially dense fur, while whales and dolphins do not have fur. Large land animals that live in hot areas, such as the elephant, have hardly any fur. Some animals have a thick winter coat and a light summer coat. Fur comes in many colors and is helpful in warming animals and providing camouflage. People also use fur and woven fabrics to help keep warm.

Possible Topics for Further Investigation

1   Some people feel strongly that animal furs should not be used to make garments for people to wear. In some cases events such as picketing or even throwing paint on people who were wearing fur coats have made headlines. With the help of a media specialist, a small group of students might be able to locate some newspaper or magazine articles that detail some antifur protests. Have the students share what they learn.

2   This book briefly mentions fur traders. Invite some students to research fur trappers and traders that were active in the United States during the eighteenth and nineteenth centuries. In which parts of the country did fur trapping take place? How were Native Americans involved in the fur trade? What was done with most of the furs that were trapped and traded? What caused this major occupation to die out? Students should report what they learn.

3   One very interesting fur is qiviut. It comes from musk oxen. Ask a pair of students to learn more about qiviut. *Oomingmak* means musk ox in the Inuit (Eskimo) language. It is also the name of the Musk Ox Producers Co-Operative at 604 H Street in Anchorage, AK 99501. Students might write to the Co-Op and ask for pamphlets describing the garments they knit from qiviut. They should be sure to include a self-addressed, stamped envelope and share what they learn with classmates.

Part II
Animals on the Farm

Animals on the Farm

● FICTION ●

- 📖 *Bearstone*
- 📖 *Big Red Barn*
- 📖 *The Haymeadow*
- 📖 *A Horse Named Sky*
- 📖 *Jim-Dandy*
- 📖 *Like Butter on Pancakes*

- 📖 *Llama in the Family*
- 📖 *Mowing*
- 📖 *Napoleon the Donkey*
- 📖 *Nothing But Trouble*
- 📖 *Sheep, Sheep, Sheep, Help Me Fall Asleep*

◆ BRIDGES AND POETRY ◆

- 📖 *All Pigs Are Beautiful*
- 📖 *A Field Full of Horses*
- 📖 *How Now, Brown Cow?*

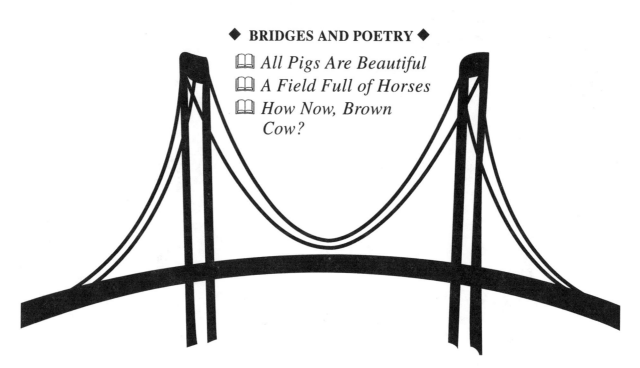

■ NONFICTION CONNECTIONS ■

- 📖 *Baby Farm Animals*
- 📖 *Calf*
- 📖 *Farming*
- 📖 *Hoofbeats, The Story of a Thoroughbred*
- 📖 *Horses*
- 📖 *Large Animal Veterinarians*

- 📖 *Milk, From Cow to Carton*
- 📖 *My Mom's a Vet*
- 📖 *Our Vanishing Farm Animals, Saving America's Rare Breeds*
- 📖 *Pig*
- 📖 *The Sheep, Farm Animal Stories*

—OTHER TOPICS TO EXPLORE—

—cattle dogs	—chickens	—4-H	—milk processing
—cattle drives	—county fairs	—geese	—rodeos
—cheese making	—FFA	—goats	—state fairs

Animals on the Farm

● *Fiction* ●

- 📖 *Bearstone*
- 📖 *Big Red Barn*
- 📖 *The Haymeadow*
- 📖 *A Horse Named Sky*
- 📖 *Jim-Dandy*
- 📖 *Like Butter on Pancakes*
- 📖 *Llama in the Family*
- 📖 *Mowing*
- 📖 *Napoleon the Donkey*
- 📖 *Nothing But Trouble*
- 📖 *Sheep, Sheep, Sheep, Help Me Fall Asleep*

 *Bearstone*

by Will Hobbs

New York: Atheneum, 1989. 154p.

 FICTION

This contemporary story is set in Colorado and is written from the point of view of a young Indian boy named Cloyd. Fourth- and fifth-grade readers will enjoy this book.

Cloyd has been in a lot of difficulty. He does not attend school and has grown up without his parents. He has lived with his grandmother and cared for goats in Utah canyons. His tribe has sent him away and Cloyd goes to spend the summer working for an old rancher.

On his first day at the ranch, Cloyd runs off and explores a ledge high above the ranch. He finds a turquoise bear in an Indian burial spot and keeps it in his pocket. He regards it as a symbol and gives himself the name Lone Bear.

On the ranch, Cloyd likes a horse that he names Blueboy. He rides the horse each day after work and dreams of going up into the high mountains.

When Cloyd and the old rancher go into the mountains to work in the man's mine, Cloyd spots a bear and feels kinship with it. He tells a hunter of seeing the bear and then feels responsible for the bear's death. When the old rancher is injured in a mine explosion, Cloyd helps rescue him. Although Cloyd has been invited to return to his tribe, he elects to remain with the old rancher and care for him until he is well enough to be on his own again.

Discussion Starters and Multidisciplinary Activities

1 Encourage students to discuss the purpose of the peach trees in this story. They play a significant part in the beginning, middle, and end of the book.

2 Cloyd has a special feeling for Blueboy, his horse, and for the bear that he meets in the mountains. Ask students to discuss what kind of attachment Cloyd has to the bear and how that is different from his feelings for Blueboy.

3 Walter has had gold fever more than once in his life. Ask students to discuss whether they think Walter will ever go back to his mine and strike it rich. What reasons can they give to support their opinion?

4 The bearstone that Cloyd finds is very beautiful. Several Indian tribes make fetishes from different types of stone. These are often crafted into lovely pieces of jewelry. A pair of students might learn more about fetishes and bring in magazine pictures and other information to share.

5 Ask a small group of students who have read the book to do geographic studies of Utah and Colorado. See if they can locate places that are mentioned in the book on the map and report what they have learned.

6 The hunter is somewhat confused about whether he has killed a black bear or a grizzly. Ask a small group of students to research both kinds of bear. Have them report orally what they have learned.

📖 *Big Red Barn* E B815b

FICTION

by Margaret Wise Brown
Illustrated by Felicia Bond
New York: HarperCollins, 1989. 32p.

The text for this book was first copyrighted in 1956 and then the book was reprinted in 1989 with new illustrations. With its simple, rhymed text and colorful pictures, this book will be enjoyed by primary-grade children.

The author describes sights and sounds on a farm, including a big red barn, a little pink pig that squeals, a big and little horse in the barn, another golden horse on the weather vane, and a pile of hay.

The sheep, donkey, geese, and goats make funny noises in the yard while the old scarecrow stands silently in the cornfield. In the barn there is a big, brown cow and a little, brown cow that are mooing. There is a noisy rooster, a pigeon, and a big white hen who is guarding a quiet egg. There is also a bantam rooster and hen with a clutch of ten eggs. Outside the barn there are cats and kittens, a dog, and puppies, all making noise.

All these different animals live together in the big, red barn and spend their days playing in the grass and hay. When the sun goes down, the animals make lowing, squealing, and braying sounds, and then, through the twilight, slowly begin walking across the field toward the barn to sleep. By the time the moon sails high in the sky, shining down on the lonely scarecrow still standing in the field, only the mice are left to play in the hay.

Discussion Starters and Multidisciplinary Activities

1 Without reading the text, flip through the book's pages from beginning to end to see if students can guess the time period the book covers. (The illustrations will show the transition from morning until night.)

2 Margaret Wise Brown says that "the children are away" and "only the animals are here today." After you have read the story, ask students to describe what a boy and girl who lived on the farm might be doing throughout the day.

3 After students have heard the whole story, ask if they can remember which animal leaves the barn at the end of the day when all the others are coming there to sleep.

4 The animals on this farm are described as making a variety of sounds. Ask for volunteers to make the sounds of the various farm animals—rooster, sheep, donkey, pig, cow, etc. Conclude with all the volunteers making their animal sounds at once!

5 One two-page illustration shows a puppy joining the kittens and a kitten joining the group of puppies. Have students write a one-page diary entry from either the point of view of a puppy who describes "my day with the cats," or from the point of view of a kitten who writes about "my day with the dogs." What would seem strange and funny?

6 If there is a farm in your area, a field trip would be a very enriching experience. After making a trip, have students write the farmer to thank him or her for the visit and to share their favorite experience on the farm.

From *Exploring the World of Animals.* © 1997. Teacher Ideas Press. (800) 237-6124.

📖 **The Haymeadow** FP285hm

FICTION

by Gary Paulsen
New York: Delacorte Press, 1992. 195p.

This contemporary story, set in Wyoming, is told from the viewpoint of fourteen-year-old John Barron. It is illustrated with a few black-and-white sketches. Readers in fourth and fifth grades will enjoy this book.

John Barron has a deep respect for his dead grandfather whom he never met. John tries to copy him in as many ways as possible and sometimes measures his father against his idealized image of his grandfather.

When a ranch hand is hospitalized, his father sends John to live alone for three months and care for six thousand sheep who will spend the summer in the haymeadow. John does not want to go. He does not know how he'll stand it out there alone with just the sheep, the dogs, the horses, the mountains, and meadow. He does not think he is ready for the responsibility.

John's worst fears are soon realized. No sooner is he left alone with the sheep than he is beset with one disaster after another. The river floods, coyotes attack, the dogs' feet are sore, and a bear injures both John and one of the dogs. It is a survival story in which one boy pits his spunk and ingenuity, and the skill of his dogs and horses, against many of the forces of nature.

When John's father comes to the haymeadow some weeks later, father and son finally have a chance to talk, to share the truth about John's grandfather, and to learn more about each other.

Discussion Starters and Multidisciplinary Activities

1   When the story begins, John Barron idealizes his grandfather but really knows very little about him. Ask readers if they were surprised about the information revealed about his grandfather toward the end of the story.

2   Through trial and error, John learned how to survive and protect the sheep in the haymeadow. Ask students to discuss what they thought John's worst ordeal was and why they thought it was the most difficult test he faced.

3   Other than a few changes of clothing, medicines, food, and cooking utensils, John took nothing special with him for the summer. Ask readers what three things they might take with them if they were setting off on such an adventure.

4   The horses and dogs in this story were very well trained. If you live in an area where resources are available, ask a knowledgeable person to visit and explain how these animals are used with sheep and how they are trained.

5   The author's wife, Ruth Wright Paulsen, supplied the sketches to illustrate *The Haymeadow*. Chapter 21, which describes the bear attack, does not contain any illustrations. Invite interested students to use any medium to prepare an illustration suitable for this chapter.

6   Ask a pair of students to find out more about Wyoming. What is its population? What are its major industries and resources? What kind of seasonal climate does it have? Invite the students to share orally what they learn.

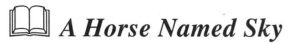

FICTION

A Horse Named Sky

by Barbara Corcoran
New York: Atheneum, 1986. 187p.

Thirteen-year old, Georgia, who has relocated in Montana tells this story. It will be enjoyed by fourth- and fifth-grade girls.

Georgia's first entry in her birthday journal is, "SOMETHING TERRIBLE HAS HAPPENED." She confides that her mother and father have been fighting again, brought about by her father losing his fourth job in two years. During this argument, her father hits her mother in the face. Georgia's older sister is away at college. Her mother has put up with enough abuse and decides to leave, taking Georgia and what they can carry in the station wagon. They move to Lolo, Montana.

Georgia is glad to have a new life, especially when she learns that in Montana she can have kittens and a horse, but Georgia does miss her old friends. Before long, she and her mother are comfortable in a small house. Her mother has found a job as a waitress, and Georgia has made friends with a girl in her new school. Georgia also becomes friendly with the Ross family that live nearby—Vera, Elmore, and Marty.

Marty brings home four mustangs and, with Georgia's help, tames one, Sky, and sells it to Georgia. Georgia's father visits near Christmas, proves he has not changed, and Georgia is relieved that they will not be returning to Massachusetts. Later Sky jumps a fence and is injured. Although Georgia loses her beloved horse, she has her music, her mother, and her new friends.

Discussion Starters and Multidisciplinary Activities

1. Because we have such a mobile society, many students will have moved and adjusted to a new school and friends. Encourage students to discuss what parts of moving are really hard and what parts are exciting and fun.

2. Georgia's new friend, Angela, is quite different from her old friend, Connie. Allow students to discuss which girl they would prefer to have for a friend and tell why. What are the major strengths and weaknesses of the two friends?

3. In this story, the horse meets an unhappy end. Let students discuss whether they would have preferred to have the story end as it does or to have Marty or the veterinarian take the horse's life.

4. Georgia has a lovely voice and is especially interested in opera. She often mentions *Madame Butterfly* and briefly describes the plot of the opera. For a group of interested students, play some of the music from this opera and discuss it.

5. In Montana, Georgia will work with a new music teacher, Mrs. Trent, who explains she will have to work hard to have a future in music. Ask a pair of students to do some research and report to the class on what local music teachers recommend as the best schools to attend after high school if one is preparing to make a career as an opera singer.

6. In some states the BLM (Bureau of Land Management) rounds up and sells wild horses. Ask a pair of students to write to the BLM and find out more about this program. Allow time for the students to share what they learn.

 *Jim-Dandy*

FICTION

by Hadley Irwin
New York: Margaret K. McElderry Books, 1994. 135p.

This is a piece of historical fiction set in Kansas after the Civil War. It is told from the viewpoint of twelve-year-old Caleb and will be enjoyed by fourth- and fifth-grade readers.

Caleb lives alone with his stepfather, Webb Cotter, on a Kansas homestead. Crops fail and there is little joy in Caleb's life until a foal, Jim-Dandy, is born, and a family moves nearby. A girl, Athens, who is about the same age as Caleb is in this family.

Webb Cotter leaves for several weeks to earn money by working on the railroad. With help from Athens, Caleb secretly begins breaking Dandy to ride.

Webb Cotter returns, but money is so scarce that he is forced to sell their only valuable possession, Dandy, to Custer's Seventh Cavalry stationed in nearby Fort Hays. The Cavalry is responsible for guarding the railroad as it is being built farther into Indian Territory.

Caleb runs away to Fort Hays. Colonel Custer's wife chooses Dandy for her own horse and Caleb is given a job as stable boy working with a man named Burke. Custer rides Dandy into a winter campaign against the Indians. Caleb knows a little sign language and once struck up a friendship with an Indian boy. Following Custer in the wagon, Caleb sees the senseless slaughter of Indians and decides to leave and take Dandy with him. But Dandy has become a cavalry horse and chooses to stay when Caleb heads for home.

Discussion Starters and Multidisciplinary Activities

1 Caleb dislikes Athens on their first meeting when she teaches him a game and he loses. Ask students to discuss their feelings for Athens at this point in the story. Did they dislike her, too? Did they guess that Caleb and Athens would eventually become good friends? What clues did they have?

2 Have students discuss Athens and her two sisters. What major role did they play in this story?

3 When the story ends, Caleb is heading for home. Have students discuss what it will be like when Caleb rejoins Webb Cotter. Will things remain the same or will recent experiences change how the two react to one another?

4 In this story, Kansas was experiencing a drought. With the help of a media specialist, have a pair of students locate monthly precipitation information for the state of Kansas for a recent year, and the same data for a second agricultural state. Have the students prepare a graph comparing monthly rainfall between the two states and share it with their class.

5 Custer led the massacre of the Cheyennes at Washita. Ask a group of students to report what they learn by researching Indians that lived in the Kansas area. What tribes lived there? What lifestyle did these tribes lead? Did these Indians end up on reservations?

6 Ask a pair of students to find out what eventually happened to Colonel Custer and to report to class what they learned about "Custer's Last Stand."

📖 *Like Butter on Pancakes*

FICTION

by Jonathan London
Illustrated by G. Brian Karas
New York: Viking, 1995. 32p.

This long poem picture book is about a day on a farm presented from a little boy's point of view. The remarkable full-page illustrations are done in soft pastels. This book, with its minimal text, will be enjoyed by primary-grade readers.

As the story begins, the spoons in the kitchen are asleep. The day's first sunlight, coming through the window, is "like butter on pancakes" spreading its warm, yellow color across the pillow of a sleeping child. A woodpecker begins tapping, and the rooster crows on the henhouse roof. The cat rolls into a pool of sunlight and begins to purr.

Then the kitchen sounds begin. The kettle whistles and bacon sizzles as slippers whisper across the kitchen floor. The little boy rubs his sleepy eyes, pulls on his bunny slippers, and dances downstairs.

After milk, pancakes, and butter, the boy licks off his milk mustache and says, "All done!" Then he dresses and runs out into the farmyard. He runs and jumps in the hay and then chases all the barnyard animals. The donkey hee-haws, the horse neighs, the geese honk, the chickens cluck, and the cow jumps over the toy truck.

After a busy day, it is time to wash up for supper. The moon comes up, and it is time for bed. Inside and outside the house, everything settles down to sleep.

Discussion Starters and Multidisciplinary Activities

1 After students have read this story, ask them which of the many colorful pictures is their favorite and why. Allow time for discussion.

2 The author uses an unusual expression several times in this story. He writes "the sun ticks." Ask students to discuss this. What usually ticks? Why does the author have the sun tick?

3 Ask students to hunt for pairs of rhyming words close together in this picture book. Allow time for students to share finds such as yellow/pillow, whistles/sizzles, shine/time, bed/head, and so on.

4 Invite students to study the pictures in this book and then write a new story to go with the pictures. In the new story, ask students to tell it from the point of view of one or more of the cats that are featured prominently throughout.

5 There are a lot of sounds in this story—a bell rings, a rooster crows, various farm animals make neighing, braying, clucking, honking sounds, a kettle whistles, bacon sizzles, and slippers whisper. Have a small group of students plan how to make these sounds. Let them record a student reading the story while the others make the appropriate sound effects and share the results.

6 To give the appearance of evening, some pictures in this book are drawn in white on a dark background. Have students draw a night scene using white chalk on a sheet of black construction paper.

📖 *Llama in the Family*

FICTION

by Johanna Hurwitz
Illustrated by Mark Graham
New York: Morrow Junior Books, 1994. 98p.

FH9491L

This story is told from the point of view of a ten-year-old boy named Adam. It is set in the country in Vermont. This book will be enjoyed by second- through fourth-grade readers.

Adam is excited when his mother hints that there may be a surprise for him when he gets home from school. Adam recently had a birthday and did not get the mountain bike that he had been hoping for. He thinks the surprise may be a new bike.

But when Adam comes home, instead of finding a new bike, he learns that a llama has been added to their family. His mother has decided to take people on short llama treks, supplying lunch and the opportunity for photographs. She hopes to make a little extra money this way.

Adam soon becomes very fond of the llama, named Ethan Allen. When school is out, he joins his mother on one of her expeditions. He is also the one to find the missing llama and Adam's young sister, April, when they go through the fence and get lost one day.

Although the business is successful, it appears that it will take a long time before there is enough money to buy Adam's bike. Adam watches ads in a New England magazine and decides to try to swap a rug for a bike. Then the opportunity comes for Adam to make a swap for a second llama. He unselfishly does so, and his father promises him a new bike before long.

Discussion Starters and Multidisciplinary Activities

1 When Adam's mother drops a hint that there will be something special when Adam gets home from school, he thought it would be a bike. Ask students what they thought it would be.

2 Ask students to discuss whether they thought Ethan Allen ruined April's birthday party or made it extra special.

3 Adam decides to make an important swap. Ask students to discuss if they have ever made a swap and if afterwards they were pleased or unhappy with the trade.

4 Adam's mother is enthusiastic about American history. She is particularly excited about history involving Vermont, including events surrounding Ethan Allen. Ask a few students to research this topic. Who was Ethan Allen? Where and when did he live? What made him famous?

5 A llama is not a typical farm animal. Invite students, with the help of the school media specialist, to find out more about llamas. Where is their native home? How are they used in their native home? Are there many llamas in the United States? What are they used for in the United States? These students should share what they learn in an oral report.

6 Each region of the country is famous for foods grown there or prepared in some special way. This story features cold blueberry soup. What kinds of foods are special and unique in your part of the world? Have students study this topic. They should pick out one favorite dish and prepare it so that classmates may taste it.

📖 *Mowing* E H 1112m

FICTION

by Jessie Haas
Illustrated by Jos. A. Smith
New York: Greenwillow Books, 1994. 26p.

This picture book, illustrated with soft watercolor and pastel drawings, will appeal to students in kindergarten through grade two. There are usually four to twelve lines of text per two-page spread.

As the story begins, Gramp and Nora go out into their field to mow early in the morning. They hear a bobolink call as they ride behind their two big farm horses. When they get to the field, Nora hops off while Gramp lowers the cutter bar and begins to mow the grass. This grass will dry in the sun and turn into hay.

Nora warns Gramp when she spies a woodchuck. She is afraid the mowing machine will cut him. But the woodchuck goes into his hole and is safe as the cutter passes by. Next Nora spies a fawn in the grass. He stays still and does not move. Gramp leaves a patch of grass standing around the fawn.

As the horses pull the mower, Nora keeps her eyes open for other animals in the fields. She sees killdeer flying over head. The birds swoop low and cry loudly. Suddenly the horses come up to a killdeer on the ground with wings spread over her nest. She will not fly, so Gramp leaves another patch of grass standing tall.

When they are finished, two patches of tall grass remain in the field. Gramp admits that some people might think they did a poor job of mowing, but he and Nora know better. Nora holds the reins and the horses head for home.

Discussion Starters and Multidisciplinary Activities

1 If any students in the class have been on a farm, invite them to share their experiences. If someone has seen hay baled, they might describe for students what happens after the mowing is complete.

2 Ask students to consider how Gramp and Nora act and how they get along in this story. By their actions, what do these two characters reveal about themselves and how they feel about each other and the world?

3 Do students think that Gramp will come back another day and mow the two patches left standing? What makes them think so?

4 Ask a pair of students to research killdeer. Have them discover what parts of the country they live in, what they eat, and how they raise their young. Have the students share their information.

5 Hay is expensive. If there is a stable nearby, invite two students to find out how much hay a horse eats in one month and how much a bale of hay costs. Ask the students to prepare six math problems based on the price of a bale of hay. When they are ready, let the class try to solve the problems.

6 The killdeer made a cry when Gramp got too near the nest. There are many CDs, tapes, and records of bird calls. If a CD, tape, or record is available, play part for the class. Let them hear the call that a killdeer makes. Play the songs and calls of other birds that are common in your area.

📖 *Napoleon the Donkey*

FICTION

by Regine Schindler
Illustrated by Eleonore Schmid
New York: Henry Holt, distributor for North South Books, 1988. 28p.

This large-format picture book has full-page color illustrations. It will be enjoyed by primary-grade readers.

Napoleon is a friendly donkey who knows everyone walking along his street. He belongs to a woman named Maria who sometimes feeds him an apple. Maria lives alone with her baby daughter. She is a weaver and makes cloth to sell in the market. With her earnings, she feeds herself, the baby, Napoleon, and buys more wool to weave.

Napoleon is even kind to a noisy crow that others would like to drive away. Napoleon always gives the crow some hay.

When Maria becomes ill, she is forced to sell Napoleon to buy food. Napoleon goes to live and work on a farm. The donkey is tired from hard work and no longer happy. The crow finds him and Napoleon gives the crow some hay as always.

Each day the crow takes hay from Napoleon and flies it to Maria. Maria sees the hay as golden threads. She recovers and begins weaving again, including the golden threads in her cloth. One day Maria carries her baby and her cloth to market. Napoleon comes to the market, too. With the money she earns from her cloth, Maria buys back her donkey. Napoleon happily returns with Maria, meets the crow and her chicks, and is happy to see Maria weaving beautiful cloth again.

Discussion Starters and Multidisciplinary Activities

1. Ask students to discuss what role they expected the crow to play in this story. Some said that crows bring bad luck. Did any students think that the crow would bring bad luck to Napoleon?

2. Have students give their interpretation of how the straw that Napoleon gave to the crow transformed into golden thread after the crow gave it to Maria.

3. The reader is not told in what country this story takes place. Let students discuss this and tell where they think the story took place and why.

4. Students may be familiar with another storybook donkey, Eeyore, from *Winnie the Pooh*. Ask a small group of students to choose a scene in which Eeyore plays a major role and present a short play to the rest of the class.

5. The full-page picture of the scene at the market would make a good class "memory game." Open the book to the market picture and put it in a spot where students can view it for one full minute. Then close the book. Ask the students to remember one thing sold in the market. List these things on the board. How many items can the class remember? Check your work with the illustration. Were some things "remembered" that were not in the picture? Were some things forgotten?

6. Napoleon is a very appealing donkey. Some students may want to use charcoal to make their own sketches of Napoleon. Share the students' artwork.

 *Nothing But Trouble*

FICTION

by Betty Ren Wright
New York: Holiday House, 1995. 119p.

This story is set on an old farm and told from the viewpoint of a young girl, Vannie Kirkland. There are a few black-and-white illustrations scattered throughout the book. It will be enjoyed by second-, third-, and fourth-grade readers.

Vannie is unhappy with being dropped off at Aunt Bert's farm while her parents travel from Cleveland to California looking for work and a new place to live. Vannie's only consolation is that her dog, a small, white poodle named Muffy, will be with her.

When Vannie meets Aunt Bert, she is miserable. Her aunt is like a tiny witch, gruff and angry, and not at all fond of dogs. Soon Vannie finds that Aunt Bert, although very direct and blunt, is kind in her own way.

Vannie is soon caught up in a mystery. Aunt Bert has leased land to a farmer, Mr. Engel, but has refused to sell any land to him. There are visitors in the night, drawings of witches on window panes, and slashed car tires.

Muffy disappears. Vannie and her new friend, April, search for the dog without success. Then one night Vannie solves the mystery when she discovers Matt Engel and Billy Barker painting rabbit ears on the huge picture of Aunt Bert's perfect dog, Josh, whose likeness was painted on the barn.

Vannie finds Muffy, but gives him away to an old lady because she will not be able to take the dog to California. She looks forward to the rest of her summer with Aunt Bert and a new puppy.

Discussion Starters and Multidisciplinary Activities

1   Knowing what they do about Aunt Bert's personality, ask students to discuss whether it would have been wiser for Vannie's parents to call ahead of time to discuss leaving Muffy and Vannie, or whether it was better to just appear on her doorstep.

2   Did the readers think that it was realistic for Vannie to be able to give up Muffy so quickly after she found her again?

3   Both Vannie and Aunt Bert underwent significant changes during the course of this book. Ask students to discuss how each character changes.

4   Outdoor murals and large sign paintings, such as the one on the barn, are a special art form. If there is a large outdoor painting in your area, invite a pair of students to find out more about it. Who painted the mural? When was it painted? What was its purpose?

5   Aunt Bert is proud of her bread and says it is not at all like store-bought bread. A few students might volunteer to try a bread recipe at home and bring it in for the class to sample. Each baker should have time to discuss how the bread-making process went and give some history about the special recipe used.

6   Two kinds of dogs were important to this story, a poodle and a golden retriever. Ask two students to research these breeds and report what they learn. What is the history of each breed? How big do the dogs grow? What special characteristics do these dogs have?

 *Sheep, Sheep, Sheep, Help Me Fall Asleep*

FICTION

by Arlene Alda
New York: Doubleday, 1992. 32p.

This rhyming tale is told in the first person. The picture book is illustrated with color photographs and will be enjoyed by primary-grade children.

As the book begins, the sleepless child telling the story is pictured tucked into bed with stuffed animals. Mommy suggests that the child look for sheep and count them.

The child sees a very itchy cow, and then a cat that is too busy to meow. Next the child sees a gorilla playing with its toes, and then five piglets playing in the mud. Although the child does not see any sheep, it is fun to see all these other animals, and the night is passing.

Next the child sees two fat hippos, and then a goat peeking out a door. Five geese appear walking in a line, followed by a horse that is neighing. The child admits to being tired of looking for sheep, but somehow still cannot get to sleep. The child wiggles, squirms, turns, and tosses.

Finally the child sees one woolly sheep, and then a pair of sheep. The child counts to three and looks for more. The child's eyelids are heavy when there are four sheep. The child counts five sheep, then six, and then seven. The child sees eight sheep grazing in a field, and then nine sheep that look as if they are hurrying toward home.

The child yawns and starts counting to ten, but there are so many sheep the child falls asleep wishing for a big kangaroo.

Discussion Starters and Multidisciplinary Activities

1 Ask students to look carefully at the first photograph showing the child in bed. We cannot tell from the picture whether the child is a boy or girl, but by looking at the child's feet, we can make some guesses about what the child was doing earlier. Ask students to discuss their ideas.

2 When the child first starts looking for sheep, there are none to be seen. The child sees many other animals instead. Ask students whether they thought the child would ever see sheep, or whether they thought the child would continue to see and count other animals.

3 The kangaroo on the last page is a surprise. Invite children to discuss the last page and suggest animals they might have put there instead of a kangaroo.

4 Some of the sheep in the photos have long hair and some have been sheared. Ask a pair of students to do some research. At what time of year are sheep sheared? Are they sheared more than once a year? Have students report what they learn to the class.

5 A group of six students might agree to write a twelve-page counting book with each student doing two animal illustrations. When the book is complete, one child might read it to a kindergarten class.

6 Ask students to write an original short story telling what the goat in the photograph is looking at from her front door and what happens to the goat. Share these stories.

◆ *Bridges and Poetry* ◆

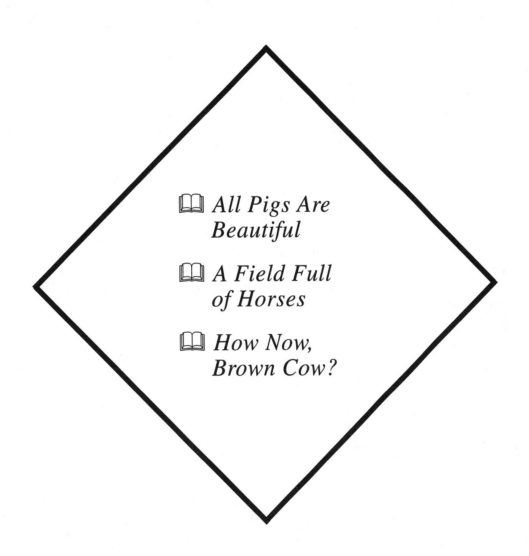

- 📖 *All Pigs Are Beautiful*

- 📖 *A Field Full of Horses*

- 📖 *How Now, Brown Cow?*

 *All Pigs Are Beautiful*

 BRIDGES AND POETRY

by Dick King-Smith
Illustrated by Anita Jeram
Cambridge, MA: Candlewick Press, 1993. 32p.

This picture book is part of a series called the Read and Wonder Books, which attempt to combine elements of exciting stories and picture-book art with elements of nonfiction, such as giving intriguing facts and ideas. For this reason, it has been chosen as a "bridge book." The simple text and colorful illustrations will appeal to primary-grade readers.

Told in the first person, the book begins by noting that the author loves all kinds of pigs, but admits that of all the pigs he has ever owned his particular favorite was a boar called Monty. (On most pages, in addition to the text of the story, some fact or bit of additional information is printed in a different type. On this page about Monty, the special type reads, "A male breeding pig is called a boar.")

Although Monty is a white pig, the author explains he does not look white because he lives outdoors and wallows in a mud hole. Monty is a gentle pig weighing six hundred pounds. Even though he is enormous, Monty likes to be scratched on the head like a dog.

Pigs like to have their backs scratched and to have people talk to them. Sows have a lot of babies and take good care of them. The author concludes that pigs are a lot like people, but while people can be plain or even ugly, all pigs are beautiful.

Possible Topics for Further Investigation

1. While studying farm animals, students can use the information that they acquire to make graphs and charts. This book notes that once a sow has been mated, the farmer expects a litter of piglets to be born three months, three weeks, and three days later. Ask a pair of students to find out how long the typical gestation period is for horses, donkeys, cows, sheep, and goats. Using this information, a group of students can list the animals' names along the horizontal axis and the gestation time in weeks along the vertical axis. They can share their graph with classmates.

2. Among all the pigs in children's literature, few are as famous or well-loved as Wilbur in *Charlotte's Web*, by E. B. White. If students in your class are not familiar with this story, you might use it as a read-aloud or share the video. As a follow-up activity, students might take a scene from the book and present it as a puppet show to another class.

3. The author of this story humorously mentions that people who do not understand what pigs are saying just hear grunts and squeaks, but that pigs might be saying all kinds of interesting things. Students will enjoy writing a short story or poem in which they interpret various animal sounds. For example, when the cow goes moo, she's saying . . .; when the kitten mews, she's really saying . . .; when the dog barks, she means. . . . Once they have finished their stories or poems, allow some time for willing students to share with each other.

📖 *A Field Full of Horses*

by Peter Hansard
Illustrated by Kenneth Lilly
Cambridge, MA: Candlewick Press, 1993. 28p.

This picture book, part of the Read and Wonder series, serves as a bridge between fiction and nonfiction. It is told in the first person, but presents a good deal of information and shows all the different parts of a horse. It will be enjoyed by primary-grade students.

The book begins with the narrator walking along a winding lane, past the willows, to a gate. There, the narrator sits to look at horses. The horses chomp grasses and the text explains that horses live outside and eat a lot of grass in summer, but are given rolled oats, barley, bran, and hay to eat during the winter months.

A section on grooming the horse identifies items such as a currycomb, dandy brush, hoof oil, sponge, hoof pick, and body brush.

A favorite horse, a mare, trots up to see if apples are available. She gives sudden shivers of her skin now and then to keep the flies away. Another horse dozes in the sun. Horses can whinny, snuffle, snicker, snort, and neigh. And they can walk, trot, canter, gallop, buck, and rear.

A two-page spread identifies all the different parts of the horse. Another two-page spread identifies different colored horses including grey, roan, bay, golden palomino, piebald, black, dun, skewbald, chestnut, and brown.

Possible Topics for Further Investigation

1 This would be a great time to arrange for a class field trip to a nearby farm or riding stable. Arrange for a time when students can observe horses being groomed. A knowledgeable person could talk about the different kinds of horses, their feeding, and care. Students should have time to ask questions. Follow up the visit with class letters thanking the expert for sharing information.

2 An art teacher could be an asset during this unit of study by using horses as the focus for art projects. Depending on their age, interest, and ability, students might sketch horses using pencil or charcoal, make wire sculptures of horses posed in various positions, or model horses from clay. If there is a safe display area in the media center, the media specialist may be willing to feature horse books and display student artwork.

3 The end of this book introduces a newborn foal who is wobbly on its feet but then quickly learns to walk. A few students may wish to combine their talents and write a picture book about a foal. One or more students may come up with a story. Another student may volunteer to proofread and divide the story into pages. A third student may be able to use a computer to print the story pages. And one or more students may make the illustrations for the story. When it is complete, perhaps a time can be arranged when one of the students can share the book with a kindergarten class.

📖 *How Now, Brown Cow?*

**BRIDGES
AND POETRY**

by Alice Schertle

Illustrations by Amanda Schaffer

New York: Harcourt Brace, Browndeer Press, 1994. 32p.

*808.1
Sch28h*

This is a book of poems about cows. Many of the poems are humorous, and most are short and rhymed. The bold illustrations are full-page and show the use of textured brush strokes in bright colors. The book is appropriate for all grades of elementary school students.

Students who are studying farm animals will enjoy this book of verse and probably be surprised that the lowly cow turned out to be the subject for an entire book of poetry. Those who have seen cows (or horses) reaching across, under, or over a fence to get at a luscious tuft of grass growing just out of reach will chuckle at "The Cow's Complaint."

When they examine the poem "Milking," students will discover that it is simply one long sentence even though it appears on the page as three stanzas of five lines each. This would be a good model for studying the function of the shape of a poem.

"Drivin' the Cows" depends partly on the words and partly on the illustration for the humor of the poem. Students will need to be familiar with two meanings of "driving" to fully appreciate it.

Humor is also an essential element of the "April 1" poem, which relies upon the ridiculousness of April Fool's Day for an understanding of the foolish things mentioned in the poem.

Discussion Starters and Multidisciplinary Activities

1 Discuss with students why the poet placed the last eight words of the poem "Clever Cows" on the page the way she did. What purpose does it serve?

2 The teacher might want to give just the title of "Drivin' the Cows," and then ask students what they think this poem might be about. After students have offered suggestions, which will probably be about cowboys on horses making a long and dusty cattle drive to market, the teacher can read the poem and share the illustration. Most students will quickly note the humor involved.

3 Read the poem, "Taradiddle," and see if students can identify the old nursery rhyme that the poem is based upon.

4 Invite students to write a "shape poem" such as the one called "Clever Cows." Encourage them to write a poem and then place the words of the poem in a way that adds to the poem's meaning.

5 After reading the poem, "Milking," ask a pair of students to find out more about the different kinds of dairy cows. What are the main dairy states and where are they located? Which are the most popular and common breeds of dairy cattle and what are their colorings and markings? Ask these students to share what they learn with the class.

6 After reading the "April 1" poem, ask students to write and illustrate their own April Fool's Day rhymes. You might want to share these on a class bulletin board.

Nonfiction Connections

📖 *Baby Farm Animals*

📖 *Calf*

📖 *Farming*

📖 *Hoofbeats, The Story of a Thoroughbred*

📖 *Horses*

📖 *Large Animal Veterinarians*

📖 *Milk, From Cow to Carton*

📖 *My Mom's a Vet*

📖 *Our Vanishing Farm Animals, Saving America's Rare Breeds*

📖 *Pig*

📖 *The Sheep, Farm Animal Stories*

📖 *Baby Farm Animals*

by Merrill Windsor

Washington, DC: National Geographic Society, 1984. 32p.

This large-format picture book describes different kinds of farms. It has simple text, is illustrated with color photographs, and will be enjoyed by primary-grade students.

A two-page spread shows several buildings on a dairy farm, as well as a small herd of cows. The milking barn where the cows are milked and the silo, where food is stored for the cows, are both discussed.

Different baby farm animals are described. Dairy calves can be born at any time of year. The cow usually has one baby, but sometimes has twins. A calf stands and walks beside its mother when it is only an hour old. The calves nurse for the first few hours, then the farmer feeds them from a bottle or a bucket.

Baby horses run with their mothers when they are only a few weeks old. The mares usually have one baby. The young are called foals until they are a year old.

A female goat, called a nanny, has babies called kids. By three weeks, kids can climb and explore. Pigs usually have big families. A whole row of piglets nurse at once.

There are many kinds of farms and ranches. Some ranches raise beef cattle while others raise dairy cattle. Most eggs come from special farms, and some farms raise turkeys.

Children who live on a farm have pets and may learn to ride horses. Other children may visit farms at a summer camp. Some young people take part in 4-H clubs and learn farming skills.

Possible Topics for Further Investigation

1   Depending on where you live, there may be an active 4-H group. If so, contact one of the adult sponsors of the group and see if you can arrange a time when the sponsor and some members can visit your class. Allow time for the sponsor and members to talk about the activities of 4-H groups. If one is raising a small animal as a 4-H project or as a fair entry, it might be possible to bring the animal to class and discuss it. If actual animals cannot be brought, perhaps the sponsor or members have photographs of some animals to share.

2   There are many farm magazines for readers who are interested in a particular subject. A few students might write to some of these magazines for a free sample, including a large, self-addressed, stamped, manila envelope. Some possibilities include: *Citrus & Vegetable Magazine*, 7402 North 56th Street, Suite 560, Tampa, FL 33617-7737; *Grain Journal*, 2490 North Water Street, Decatur, IL 62526; *The Western Dairyman*, Dept. WM, P.O. Box 819, Corona, CA 91718-0819; *Llamas Magazine*, P.O. Box 100, Herald, CA 95638; and *National Lamb Wool Grower*, 6911 South Yosemite Street, Englewood, CO 80112-1414. Share the magazines with classmates.

3   A pair of students might prepare a word game for two teams of students to play. A card is revealed, such as "nanny," and the team member who first says "kid" wins the card. To play, students will have to prepare pairs of cards with names given to mother and baby animals such as mare/foal, sow/piglet, goose/gosling, ewe/lamb, kangaroo/joey, and so on.

 *Calf*

by Mary Ling
Photographs by Gordon Clayton
New York: Dorling Kindersley, 1993. 21p.

This picture book will appeal to students in kindergarten through second grade. It is part of a series called See How They Grow.

A young calf tells its story as it grows to two years of age, providing the reader information along the way. First, the newborn calf tries to stand on its weak and wobbly legs and stays near its mother, a Jersey cow.

As it grows older, the little calf enjoys special treats to eat. The farmer's wife feeds her and she likes eating lots of grass that she pulls up with her rough tongue. She also plays with the other calves.

In the barn, the calf talks with the rooster. The calf likes staying in the barn because it is warm and smells sweet there. When the calf is ten months old, she goes to the meadow to graze. Gradually her coat changes color until the calf looks like the older cows.

By the time the calf has grown up and is fourteen months old, a baby calf is growing inside her. She continues to eat a lot of grass to nourish her baby.

When the story ends, the original calf is now two years old. She has her own baby calf, which she feeds with her warm milk. She also goes to the milking barn where the farmer milks her as part of his dairy herd.

Possible Topics for Further Investigation

1. Cows eat a lot of grass. Grass and grazers go together. The cow eats off the tips of grass, and the grass keeps growing. If grasslands are grazed too heavily by too many animals, the grass is cut so short that it can no longer grow. A pair of students might be interested in finding out more about grasslands. They could write to the Pawnee National Grasslands, 2009 9th Street, Greeley, CO 80631 and request pamphlets. With their request, students should enclose a large, stamped, self-addressed envelope. They should share any information that they receive with classmates.

2. Milk from dairy cattle is available to consumers in many forms—homogenized, pasteurized, and skim. Have a small group of students learn more about how milk is treated and prepared. When they understand and can explain the processes, allow time for them to share their information.

3. Students like to make and solve word puzzles. Invite a small group of students to prepare word scrambles for the rest of the class. Have the students prepare the scrambled word list on a computer so that the teacher can make copies. The students making the puzzle should also prepare and print an answer key. All of the scrambled words should have something to do with a farm. Possible examples of easy words include: yidra/dairy, flac/calf, limgink/milking. A tougher word list might include ruzipasteed/pasteurized.

 *Farming*

by Brian Williams
Austin, TX: Raintree Steck-Vaughn, 1993. 48p.

This is one volume of a four-volume series called Ways of Life. Each book examines ways that people have earned their living over the centuries. The book is illustrated with color photographs and will be enjoyed by third- through fifth-grade readers. It contains a glossary and index.

This book is divided into five chapters, "The Key to Civilization," "The Business of Farming," "Farmers of Long Ago," "Farming Today," and "Farming in the Modern World." The first chapter explains that farming is the world's most important industry because farming makes it possible for people to build cities and towns and stay in one place without wandering and hunting for food. Although farmers produce more and more food, two-thirds of the world's people are undernourished.

There are rich and poor farmers, but they share a common bond to the land. Farmers know the weather and seasons, put up with pestilence and drought, and must find markets for their products.

In the chapter, "Farmers of Long Ago," there are sections on farming in Egypt, China, Greece, Rome, Europe during the Middle Ages, and early American colonies.

Farming today takes place on specialized farms and produce may be sold to people thousands of miles away. Although in some countries farming has changed little, in most places farms have increased greatly in size, and there are fewer farm workers and much more specialized machinery.

Possible Topics for Further Investigation

1 Cotton, tobacco, sugarcane, and other crops are grown on southern plantations. Starting in the 1640s, many workers on these plantations were slaves brought from Africa. Until the mid-1800s, slaves were bought and sold by white masters. A small group of students may be interested in studying this topic. Why were slaves used in the south? Why did the New England states not rely on slavery as heavily as southern states? What political figures were significant in calling an end to slavery in the United States? These students should share what they learn.

2 The Dust Bowl was an important part of American history. Ask a small group of students to research the Dust Bowl and make an oral presentation. During their presentation, the students should use a map of the United States and point out which states were most affected. They should also explain when the Dust Bowl occurred, how long it lasted, and what farming techniques are used today to try to make sure a dust bowl does not occur again.

3 Bangladesh is a very poor farming country with more than 104 million people. Rice is a major crop, but they have a terrible flooding problem. Cyclones rush in from the Bay of Bengal and drive the sea inland. Have a pair of students research this and share information with the class. When did the last major flooding in Bangladesh occur? Students should point out both Bangladesh and the Bay of Bengal on a world map.

📖 *Hoofbeats, The Story of a Thoroughbred*

by Cynthia McFarland
New York: Atheneum, 1993. 32p.

NONFICTION CONNECTIONS

This book has a simple text and each page is illustrated with a color photograph. It will be enjoyed by second-through fourth-grade readers.

This story is set at Silver Meadows Farm where there are horses grazing and dozing in fields, waiting in stalls, and galloping around the training track. The horses are thoroughbreds who can run up to forty-five miles an hour.

When raising thoroughbreds, the owner chooses a broodmare and a stallion based on their builds, conformation, and pedigree. The broodmare carries an unborn foal for about eleven months and then has a male foal, called a colt, or a female foal, called a filly. In this story, the mare has a dark colt. Although the colt is wobbly when it is first born, it is able to run later that day.

The colt and his mother spend their first days in a paddock. The colt gets milk from its mother and begins to grow teeth at the end of a week so that he can eat grass and nibble grain.

Every six weeks the blacksmith trims the colt's hooves. Trimming makes it more likely that the colt's legs will grow straight. The horses are brushed every day. By six months, the colt, named Sailor, is weaned from its mother. Sailor begins race training just before he turns two. He gets used to a saddle, bit, and rider. Gradually he learns to gallop and to stand in the starting gate. Then Sailor travels to his first race where he comes in second.

Possible Topics for Further Investigation

1 Even people who know little about horses and do not own or ride them may watch or read about a few races each year. Some races are big sporting events that are televised. A Triple Crown winner identifies one horse that wins three of the year's biggest horse racing events. This rarely happens. With the help of a media specialist, invite a pair of students to learn more about the Triple Crown. What are the three races? How much prize money did the winner earn last year at one of these races? When and where are they run each year? What horses throughout history have won the Triple Crown?

2 On an 18-x-24-inch canvas board, have a small group of students draw an oval racetrack divided into two-inch squares. A few of the squares might give directions such as, "horse nervous, drop back two spaces," or "throws a shoe, return to start." Then find five small plastic horses to serve as markers. Students may race each other to see who wins. A die is thrown, and the horse advances the number shown *if the player* can correctly spell the contraction for two words shown on the top card in a pile of cards. The correct answer is on the back of each card. (Is not - isn't, have not - haven't, I would - I'd, and so on.)

3 Many students are fascinated with sporting records. Thoroughbred horse racing is filled with all kinds of records. Have a student research this topic and make a chart of interesting racing records, posting it where classmates can study it.

 ## *Horses*

by Dorothy Hinshaw Patent
Minneapolis: Carolrhoda Books, 1994. 48p.

**NONFICTION
CONNECTIONS**

This book is part of a series, Understanding Animals. It is illustrated with color photographs and will be enjoyed by readers in fourth and fifth grades. It is divided into four chapters and contains a glossary and index.

The reader learns that horses are one of the most recent animals to have been domesticated and that they have changed little from their wild ancestors. Since prehistoric times, horses have been a source of labor for people.

There are many kinds of horses. Miniatures stand less than 34 inches tall at the shoulder. Ponies grow to 58 inches tall. Saddle horses and thoroughbreds are big enough to carry a saddle and an adult. And Clydesdales and Percherons stand 72 inches at the shoulder and may weigh over a ton.

Prehistoric horses were probably hunted for meat. At some time, perhaps between 4500 and 2500 BC horses were being tamed in Europe and Asia. By 1000 BC horses were used for pulling wagons and chariots in North Africa, Europe, and Asia.

Today there are no truly wild horses in North or South America, but there are feral horses, domesticated horses that have gone wild. Both feral and domestic horses are social and like to band together. In the wild, horses spend most of their time grazing and need about twenty-five pounds of grass each day. Horses communicate through whinnies and neighs. In the western world today, most horses are used for pleasure rather than for work.

Possible Topics for Further Investigation

1   A group of students may want to do research on feral horses and report what they learn to the class. The Bureau of Land Management (BLM) is the government agency that manages most of the lands where wild horses live in the United States. They are responsible for about 50,000 wild horses. Students may want to write to the BLM asking for information about wild horses and roundups they hold when an area becomes overpopulated. What procedure is used to adopt one of these wild horses and what is the adoption center closest to you?

2   Horses in the western world today are used mostly for pleasure. Some are bred and trained for racing, and there are many different kinds of racing. *Hoof Beats* is a monthly magazine that covers the sport of harness racing. A small group of students may want to learn more about harness racing and report what they learn. To obtain a free sample copy of this magazine, write and include an 11-x-13-inch, stamped, self-addressed envelope to *Hoof Beats*, United States Trotting Association, 750 Michigan Avenue, Columbus, OH 43215.

3   Horses are such popular animals among students that they would make a good topic for a class bulletin board. Each student could submit something for the project—an original short story featuring a horse, a horse poem, sketches or paintings of horses, a report about a particular breed or horse-related topic, a chart showing winners of the Kentucky Derby, a crossword puzzle with horse-related words, etc.

📖 *Large Animal Veterinarians*

NONFICTION CONNECTIONS

by Rod Bellville and Cheryl Walsh Bellville
Minneapolis: Carolrhoda Books, 1983. 32p.

This picture book is illustrated with black-and-white photographs. It will be enjoyed by second- through fourth-grade readers.

The author begins by explaining that veterinarians are doctors who do for animals what medical doctors do for people. A large animal veterinarian treats horses, dairy and beef cattle, sheep, pigs, and wildlife.

Large animal veterinarians travel to their patients in cars and trucks filled with their equipment and with a pharmacy of pills, vaccines, and other drugs. These vets are on call seven days a week and at all hours of the day and night.

Each morning the vet plans the stops for the day and calls to an office on a car radio to see if there are any emergencies or other needed stops. Because animals cannot talk and tell the veterinarian about their pains and discomfort, the doctor must rely on observation to diagnose problems.

Large animals receive maternity care, emergency care to treat accidents and sickness, and preventive care to help keep animals from getting sick. Some large animal veterinarians spend most of their time with dairy or beef cattle. Others specialize in the care of pigs, horses, and sheep. A large animal veterinarian may also vaccinate dogs or other pets during a farm visit.

Students attend veterinary school for at least three years after they have completed college.

Possible Topics for Further Investigation

1 The training to become a veterinarian is similar to that required to be a medical doctor. To compare and contrast the two, invite a local veterinarian and a pediatrician to visit your class. Have students prepare a list of questions ahead of time. Each doctor might explain the following: Where did you go to school? How long did your studies take? What subjects did you study? What sorts of vaccinations do you commonly give your patients? Once you begin your practice, do you take any more training? After the visit, be sure that students send a thank-you letter to their guests.

2 Page 22 of this book introduces what may be a new word for students, zoonosis. It is a term for any disease that is common to both animals and people. One such disease is rabies. Invite a small group of students to research rabies. How do animals and people contract rabies? Is there a treatment for animals with rabies? Is there a treatment for people with rabies? What is done when a rabid animal bites a human? Once they have finished their research, the students should share their information.

3 Some pictures in this book show veterinarians giving routine vaccinations. Most students in your class will have had routine DPT shots. (Be aware that some students may have declined shots for personal or religious reasons.) Ask a pair of interested students to find out and report what DPT shots are for and how often they are needed.

📖 *Milk, From Cow to Carton*

by Aliki Brandenberg

637 Al44m

New York: HarperCollins, 1992. 32p.

This is part of the Let's-Read-and-Find-Out Science Book series. The text is simple and the clever illustrations are a combination of ink, watercolors, and pencil crayons. It will be enjoyed by primary-grade students.

In explaining how milk gets from cow to carton, the book begins with cows in late spring and summer grazing in good pastures in the mountains, valleys, fields, and meadows. At this time, farmers also cut grass and dry it in the sun so that they will have hay to feed the cattle during the cold months of the year. Good food is important because the better a cow eats, the better the milk she will give.

Although some farmers milk their cows by hand, farmers with many cows use machines to milk faster. The milk is pumped through tubes into a covered pail. This raw milk is stored in a refrigerated tank. A refrigerated tanker takes the milk to a dairy where the raw milk is processed. Milk is stored in big tanks and there are machines to homogenize and pasteurize the milk. There are other machines that put the milk into bottles and cartons.

Flat cartons are put in one machine. The cartons are opened, heated, and the bottoms are sealed. Milk is put into the cartons, then the top of the carton is heated and sealed. The cartons are dated, stacked in cases, moved to a refrigerated room, and then taken by truck to their destination.

Possible Topics for Further Investigation

1. A pair of students may be interested in making a large display chart. The information given on page 11 of this book will be helpful. The students should explain that a cow has four stomachs—Rumen, Reticulum, Omasum, and Abomasum. These should be shown on a large drawing. The students should research the topic so that they will be able to explain to classmates the function of each of the four stomachs and the way in which part of the food is made into milk.

2. The text explains that a contented dairy cow gives thirty quarts of milk a day. This information can be the basis for a number of practical math problems. Invite a small group of students to prepare some math problems to solve using this information. For example, if the school cafeteria daily serves one-half pint of milk to 500 students, how many dairy cows supply the school with milk for a week?

3. It is very important that a dairy is kept very clean and that milk is refrigerated all along the way. A student may wish to do a simple science experiment with milk and half-and-half. The student should pour one inch of milk into two plastic glasses and one inch of half-and-half into another two plastic glasses. Each glass should be dated on a piece of tape. Two glasses should be marked "refrigerated" and stored in the refrigerator. Two should be marked "unrefrigerated" and left on a kitchen counter. The student should check all four glasses twice a day, make notes, and report back what happens.

 *My Mom's a Vet*

**NONFICTION
CONNECTIONS**

by Henry Horenstein
Cambridge, MA: Candlewick Press, 1994. 62p.

This large-format book is illustrated with color photographs and will be enjoyed by students in grades two through five. It is told in the first person, from the point of view of a young girl, Darcie, whose mother is a veterinarian. This particular veterinarian drives around to different farms to care for large animals such as cows and horses. Darcie is spending one week of her summer vacation working with her mother as an assistant.

In simple text, the job of a farm veterinarian is explained. The first animal to be examined, Elmo, needs an exam before he can be sold and moved out of state. After the exam, the veterinarian fills out a certification form verifying Elmo's good health.

It is emphasized that veterinarians need beepers and cellular phones twenty-four hours a day since emergencies frequently arise.

During the course of the book, the veterinarian visits a riding horse that has a fractured leg diagnosed with X rays taken on the spot, helps a cow deliver her first calf, dehorns a seven-day-old goat, vaccinates a sow with piglets, cares for a horse with an injured eye, examines pregnant cows, cleans up the leg wound of a goat, and operates on a cow with a twisted stomach. Each procedure is presented in a matter-of-fact way and in sufficient detail so that the reader gets a clear picture of the variety of work done by a veterinarian specializing in farm animals.

Possible Topics for Further Investigation

1 This book provides an excellent opportunity to learn more about the work of a veterinarian by asking a local veterinarian to visit the class and talk about his or her work. A pair of students might coordinate the invitation to the veterinarian. These same students might prepare six questions that they would like to have answered during the visit. Use care to select a time that will work for everyone and clearly specify details—length of talk, address of school, teacher's name, and grade level. After the visit, the two students should also have the responsibility of writing a follow-up thank-you letter.

2 This book notes that if animals are being sold or moved out of state, certificates are needed. Ask a small group of students to find out more about this process. Why are certificates required? Are certificates only required for farm animals? Do different states have different laws and requirements? The students should report what they learn.

3 The veterinarian in this story uses a beeper and a cellular phone so that she can be easily contacted. Invite someone from the telephone company to visit your class to explain how a beeper and a cellular phone work. How are they different from an ordinary telephone? Students should be in charge of making the arrangements for the visit and following up with a thank-you letter after the visit.

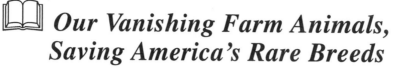 *Our Vanishing Farm Animals, Saving America's Rare Breeds*

NONFICTION CONNECTIONS

by Catherine Paladino

Boston: Little, Brown, 1991. 32p.

This book is illustrated with excellent color photographs and will be enjoyed by readers in third through fifth grade. The book tells stories of small family farms where rare breeds of animals still exist.

Most readers think of exotic animals when they consider animals facing extinction. This book points out that over half of our breeds of farm animals currently exist in such small numbers that they could become extinct.

Modern commercial farms tend to focus on animals that are used for a single purpose, such as giving the most meat, wool, milk, and so on. But older breeds of animals tended to be used for many purposes. Red devon cattle were raised for their cream, milk, and meat, and also pulled the farmer's plow.

Some of these older breeds of animals came to America with settlers and traders from other countries. Although the older breeds do not produce as much as the modern breeds, the older ones required less food and shelter and are especially hardy. They also can survive on low-quality forage.

Among the breeds of farm animals discussed in this book are the Dutch belted cow, the Gloucester old spot pig, the Guinea hog, the Navajo-Churro sheep, the American mammoth jackstock, Ancona and black Australorp chickens, and the American bashkir curly horse.

Possible Topics for Further Investigation

1. This book gives the address of the American Minor Breeds Conservancy, P.O. Box 477, Pittsboro, NC 27312 as a source of information about farm animals that are in danger of extinction. Ask a pair of students to write the rough draft of a letter requesting information. Have student editors critique the rough draft and check spelling and punctuation, as well as making other suggestions for improvement. After students write a final copy, they should send it, including a stamped, self-addressed envelope for return information.

2. Three kinds of goats are in danger of extinction. Ask a few interested students to research and report what they learn about Fainting goats, Nigerian dwarf goats, and San Clemente goats. Why is each type of goat valuable? Where is it found? What problems does it currently face? With the help of a media specialist, see if students can find pictures of the three types of goats to bring to class when they make their report.

3. Churro wool is discussed in the book. It is used for rugs, jackets, and pillows. Invite a weaver who can set up a loom and demonstrate how wool is woven into cloth. As a follow-up to this guest artist, invite the art specialist at your school to help the students set up a weaving project. This might be done on a free standing loom on which students could take turns on a class weaving or might be done on individual small hand looms.

 *Pig*

by Mary Ling
Photographs by Bill Ling
New York: Dorling Kindersley, 1993. 21p.

Readers in kindergarten through second grade will enjoy this picture book. It is part of a series of books called See How They Grow. The information is presented from a pig's point of view.

As the story begins, the piglet, and its six brothers and sisters, have just been born. They squeak and squeal because they are wet and cold. Their legs are wobbly, but they soon find their mother. She lies down and snorts when it is time for the piglets to drink her warm milk.

The piglets grow quickly, and every day they are bigger. When the wind blows into their sty, they all snuggle together to keep warm. By the time they are two weeks old, they like to trot around the farmyard and sometimes follow the farmer to the gate. They sleep in a soft straw nest.

By the time the pigs are six weeks old, they eat from a trough just like the older pigs. By the time they are six months old, the pigs are getting big. They like to play in the cool and sloshy mud.

When the original piglet has grown to be one year and six months old and is a full-grown pig, she has eight little piglets of her own. She takes good care of them and is careful not to step on them. She knows that one day these little piglets will be as big and strong as she is now.

Possible Topics for Further Investigation

1 A small group of students may wish to present *The Three Little Pigs* as a puppet show for a kindergarten class. The pig puppets may be made by stuffing small lunch sacks with crumpled paper and tying them closed. The tied end can become the pig's snout. A pink yarn tail and pink construction paper ears can be added, and eyes drawn on. A dowel stick can be pushed into the sack and held in place to serve as a handle. The houses of straw, sticks, and bricks can be drawn and pinned to a background curtain of the puppet stage. Students may want to tape-record their roles and run the tape during the show so that they can concentrate on the operation of the puppets.

2 There are lots of expressions that use traits of animals, such as busy as a bee, sly as a fox, cross as a bear, and eats like a pig. A pair of students might want to write and illustrate a short picture book based on these animal expressions. Allow time for the students to share their completed book.

3 Many animals, including pigs, are judged at county and state fairs. If you live in an area where these agricultural fairs take place, contact a fair official and ask for the name of one of the local judges of pigs. Invite that person to visit and discuss judging. What does this judge look for when pigs are shown at the fair? How long has the person served as a fair judge? What background gives him or her the knowledge needed for judging?

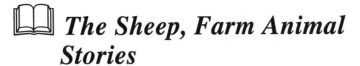

The Sheep, Farm Animal Stories

NONFICTION CONNECTIONS

by Angela Royston
Illustrated by Josephine Martin
New York: Warwick Press, 1990. 24p.

This is one of a series of six titles called Farm Animal Stories. The text is simple and the illustrations are in full-color. This book will be enjoyed by primary students.

As the book begins, it is summertime and the sheep are grazing high up in the hills. A strange dog barks and frightens one of the sheep who slides down a slope and gets stuck on a rocky ledge. That night, the sheepdog and shepherd find the sheep who is bleating, and they help her to return to her lamb and the other sheep.

In fall, the sheep are moved downhill and driven into a pen in the farmyard. Each is inspected and is dipped in a special bath to kill off ticks and insects in the wool.

In winter, the rams and sheep mate. The ground is covered in frost and the sheep have trouble finding enough to eat. When it snows, the shepherd comes and throws bales of hay to the sheep. He moves them to a field nearer to the farm.

In the spring, the lambs are born. The lambs are wobbly on their legs at first, but then they stand and drink their mother's milk. In another month, the lambs are nibbling grass and playing with other lambs.

In summer, the shepherd uses electric shears to cut wool from the sheep. All summer long the sheep and the lambs graze back up on the hills.

Possible Topics for Further Investigation

1   The sheep in this story are Welsh Mountain sheep. Other hill sheep include blackfaces and cheviots. Lowland sheep are texel sheep and Oxford downs. Merinos give the best wool and are most popular in the United States. Ask a few interested students to research sheep. They can chart information listing the sheep's name, where it is commonly found, and include a drawing or picture of the sheep to help identify it.

2   Wool is valued in clothing because of its great insulating qualities. A student may carry out a science experiment to demonstrate the insulating qualities of wool. Fill three bottles with hot tap water. Take the temperature of the water in the bottles. Wrap one bottle in cotton cloth, wrap one bottle in wool cloth, and leave the third bottle unwrapped. Place all three bottles in a cool place. Wait one hour. Then take the temperature of the water in all three bottles again. The water in the bottle wrapped in wool should be the warmest because wool is a good insulator.

3   The Navajos are Native Americans who are famous as sheepherders. Ask a pair of interested students to research Navajos. Where did they once live in large numbers? Where do they live today? For what purposes do they use sheep? Can the students locate a small rug or blanket made by Navajos that they might bring in to share with the class? Students should orally report what they learn.

Part III
Animals in the Woods

Clare Miller

Animals in the Woods

● FICTION ●

- 📖 *The Bear*
- 📖 *Crow and Weasel*
- 📖 *The Deer Stand*
- 📖 *Forest*
- 📖 *In the Woods: Who's Been Here?*

- 📖 *Mole's Hill: A Woodland Tale*
- 📖 *Prairie Dog Town*
- 📖 *Return of the Wolf*
- 📖 *The Spring Rabbit*
- 📖 *A Week of Raccoons*
- 📖 *Wolf at the Door*

◆ BRIDGES AND POETRY ◆

- 📖 *Wild Voices*
- 📖 *Winter's Orphans: The Search for a Family of Mountain Lion Cubs*
- 📖 *Birds, Beasts, and Fishes: A Selection of Animal Poems*

■ NONFICTION CONNECTIONS ■

- 📖 *Amazing Bears*
- 📖 *Busy Beavers*
- 📖 *I See Animals Hiding*
- 📖 *The Case of Mummified Pigs: And Other Mysteries in Nature*
- 📖 *Cottontails, Little Rabbits of Field and Forest*

- 📖 *Playful Slider, The North American River Otter*
- 📖 *Meet the Moose*
- 📖 *Wolves*
- 📖 *The Wonder of Wolves*
- 📖 *Wonders of Foxes*
- 📖 *The World of Squirrels*

—OTHER TOPICS TO EXPLORE—

—badgers	—ferrets	—lynx	—opossums
—chipmunks	—grizzlies	—moose	—skunks
—coyotes	—hunting licenses	—national parks	—wolverines

● *Fiction* ●

- 📖 *The Bear*
- 📖 *Crow and Weasel*
- 📖 *The Deer Stand*
- 📖 *Forest*
- 📖 *In the Woods: Who's Been Here?*
- 📖 *Mole's Hill: A Woodland Tale*
- 📖 *Prairie Dog Town*
- 📖 *Return of the Wolf*
- 📖 *The Spring Rabbit*
- 📖 *A Week of Raccoons*
- 📖 *Wolf at the Door*

 *The Bear*

FICTION

by Raymond Briggs
New York: Random House, 1994. 40p.

This is an unusual and extra-large-format book that will be a good read-aloud for kindergarten and first-grade students, as well as a book that students will enjoy reading in second and third grades. Some sections contain full-page pictures, while other pages are divided into a dozen smaller-sized pictures and contain a lot of text. The pictures are done in soft pastels.

One night after Tilly and her teddy bear go to bed, a big white bear climbs in the window and joins them in Tilly's house. Tilly loves her new friend, but soon finds that having a bear around means a lot of work. She has to clean up after him and try to feed him. The bear also has a habit of disappearing. While Tilly tries to make the bear comfortable and reports her progress to her parents, mother and father believe that the whole thing is a figment of Tilly's imagination.

Tilly tries to get the bear to settle down in the guest room, but he prefers to go into Tilly's parents' room instead. While he sleeps, others in the house keep quiet so as not to wake him. That evening, Tilly explains to her mother that the bear is under her bed. When mother leaves, Tilly encourages the bear to come out and sleep with her. But that night, he creeps out the window and leaves as quietly as he came.

Tilly's father consoles her and explains that it is for the best because bears cannot really live in houses with people. Tilly is left once again with her teddy bear for company.

Discussion Starters and Multidisciplinary Activities

1 Some students may argue that this whole story is a dream. Other students may think that the bear really came, was seen by no one but Tilly, and left the same way he came. Still others will think that Tilly imagined the whole story. Allow students to express opinions and try to support them with evidence from the story.

2 The story does not explain what mother does. Ask students to guess mother's occupation and explain why they think as they do.

3 Tilly sleeps with a favorite toy bear. Ask children to talk about their favorite stuffed animals. The teacher might want to designate a special day when any willing student can bring and share a favorite stuffed animal.

4 Mother makes a guess that the visitor is a polar bear. Tilly gives the bear milk and honey. Ask a pair of students to discover and report to the class what polar bears usually eat.

5 Polar bears are huge. Ask a small group of students to research the size and weight of polar bears and to use the data to prepare a few math problems for the class to solve. For example, given the average height of a male polar bear in feet, how many inches tall is he? Convert the average male polar bear height from feet to meters.

6 Ask a small group of students to research where the natural habitats of polar bears are found. Using a large map of the world, have these students show their classmates where polar bears live in the wild.

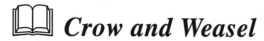

📖 *Crow and Weasel*

FICTION

by Barry Lopez

FL881c

Illustrations by Tom Pohrt

San Francisco: North Point Press, 1990. 63p.

This large-format book contains mostly text but has a few lovely full-color illustrations. The story is set in "myth time" when people and animals spoke the same language, and it is similar in tone to Native American stories. It will be enjoyed by readers in third and fourth grades.

This is a novella-length fable and is very unusual in its construction. Although the story and pictures depict various animals of the woods, the actions and garments suggest that they are part of a Native American tribe.

The story begins with two young travelers, Crow and Weasel, setting out on horseback to travel farther north than any of their people have gone before. Although they have permission of Mountain Lion to make the journey, their families are opposed. They cross the River of Floating Ashes, go through a deep forest, and go around a maze of lakes. Crow and Weasel are welcomed by Eskimos in their hunting camp, and they share stories.

As Crow and Weasel travel together, their friendship grows. They encounter danger and they also see great natural beauty. Along the way they meet Mouse, Badger, and Grizzly Bear.

They also learn lessons, such as how to behave as a friend and the necessity of giving thanks. They discover how trying to respect and understand the ways of others is crucial in finding one's own place in the world.

Discussion Starters and Multidisciplinary Activities

1 Invite students to discuss why the author chose a crow and weasel to be the central characters of this book. They ride horses and dress like Native Americans. How would the story be different if two Native American boys were the main characters?

2 On page 19, Crow gives some advice. He says that while a young man wants to fight everything, a grown man knows to leave certain things alone. Encourage students to discuss this section. Is this a piece of wisdom? Do students agree with it?

3 Many gifts are exchanged during the story, for example, Badger gives Crow and Weasel each a winter robe of buffalo, and they give her a beaded bag. Of all the gifts exchanged, which do the students think was of most value, and why?

4 It is a flicker that is chosen to lead Crow and Weasel on part of their journey. Ask a pair of students to research flickers and share what they learn. The students should find a picture to share that shows the bright orange color of the flicker's outspread wings.

5 Page 24 explains how Crow and Weasel made something to eat called pemmican. This is a food that mountain men of the west also made. Invite a small group of interested students to research pemmican. What is it? Who used it, and why?

6 As the book ends, Crow and Weasel are invited to tell their friends and relatives about their long journey. Ask two students, one to be Crow and one Weasel, to invent a story about part of the journey described in this book.

📖 The Deer Stand

FM 759d

FICTION

by Ann M. Monson

New York: Lothrop, Lee & Shepard, 1992. 171p.

This story is told from the point of view of a middle-school girl named Bits, who has just moved from Chicago to northwestern Wisconsin. It will be enjoyed by fourth- and fifth-grade readers.

Bits hates Wisconsin. She misses all of her friends and the bustle of city life. She is lonely in the new school where no one speaks to her and some girls seem to be making fun of her.

Bits often goes into the woods near her home. There she spies a beautiful young deer that she names Buck. Each day when it is possible, Bits goes to a platform and ladder that she has discovered in the woods and looks for Buck. She brings him apples, carrots, and corn, and gradually tames him.

Bits also makes a friend, Chris, at school and invites her over to meet Buck.

Chris informs Bits that the platform in the woods is a deer stand where hunters will soon come to kill deer. Bits shares her secret about taming the deer with her parents and tries several unsuccessful approaches to try to get Buck to be afraid of humans again. Then she decides to build a pen and keep Buck there for the sixteen days of hunting season.

Bits is appalled to learn that Chris and her family are hunters, but comes to realize that some hunters obey laws and are respectful of game, while others do not. Buck gets out of the pen and is wounded by a hunter. Bits and Chris find the deer, dying and in pain. Chris goes to get her brother, Jeremy, and at Bits' request, Chris kills the deer to end its pain.

Discussion Starters and Multidisciplinary Activities

1. Several characters in the book do not believe in killing game animals and are unable to shoot even when they have an animal in a gun sight. Chris, on the other hand, enjoys hunting. Discuss with students how they feel about deer hunting.

2. Bits has a hard time adjusting to the new school. Several students in class may also have had the experience of moving from one school to another. Allow them to discuss how they felt and what sorts of actions made them feel unwelcome or welcome.

3. Chris has an older brother and Bits has a younger brother. Ask students if they could choose, would they rather have an older or younger brother. Why?

4. States have different laws that govern hunting. In some states, hunters use guns and in others can use bows and arrows. In some states, it is legal to kill does and in others only bucks. Ask a pair of students to research the laws governing deer hunting in your state and share the information, including how they carried out the research.

5. Several different kinds of deer are native to the United States. Ask a group of students to research this topic. What kinds of deer live in the United States? Where are they found? Bring pictures showing the different deer.

6. This book lacks illustrations. Ask an interested student to illustrate the passage showing how the characters looked on Halloween night when they went trick-or-treating. Post the picture on a class bulletin board.

 *Forest*

by Janet Taylor Lisle

New York: Orchard Books, 1993. 150p.

FL689f

FICTION

This book blends realistic fiction and animal fantasy. The main character is twelve-year-old Amber Padgett. Readers in grades three through five will enjoy this book.

Amber has run away from home before. She does this when all the injustices of the world seem to pile up and she needs time to think. As the story begins, Amber has run to the woods not far from home, taking a sleeping bag and supplies with her. She climbs high up in the trees and is observed by mink-tailed squirrels, especially one named Woodbine. Woodbine and Amber recognize the intelligence in one another's eyes and wish they could speak to each other.

Amber's father leads an unsuccessful search party, becomes aware of masses of squirrels, and, upset and angry, takes his gun and fires into the trees at them. He kills some squirrels and almost hits Amber who is sitting up in her perch.

Amber's father organizes a search and destroy mission against the squirrels. At the same time, the squirrels decide to declare war on the humans for invading their trees, shooting at them, and taking a wounded squirrel, Brown Nut, prisoner.

Amber and her brother, Wendell, seek the help of Professor Spark in restoring peace to the forest. At the same time, Woodbine, Laurel, and Brown Nut seek out the elders among the squirrels and convince them to reassert their authority, end the war, and banish the power hungry Commander Barker.

Discussion Starters and Multidisciplinary Activities

1. Mr. Padgett does not seem to understand either of his two children very well. Ask students to find passages in the book that demonstrate how little he understands Amber and Wendell. Will he understand them better after the war with the squirrels?

2. Woodbine is always being scolded for not attending to squirrel business, yet he is instrumental in bringing the squirrel war to an end. Ask students to discuss what role they think Woodbine will play among the squirrels in the future.

3. When the story ends, there are plans among both squirrels and humans for more contact and study of one another. Do you think anything will come of Professor Spark's future studies?

4. There are many varieties of squirrels. One of the most interesting is the Douglas squirrel, found in the Sierras and in the Hoh Rain Forest in Washington. Ask a small group of students to research the Douglas squirrel and report what they learn. How big is this squirrel? What is its major food supply? What does its nest look like?

5. Amber thinks she can almost understand the chattering of the squirrels. Some research projects in communicating with apes have been successful. Have a pair of students enlist the help of a media specialist to find some magazine articles about these communication projects.

6. Ask students to draw one or more of the central characters in the book (human or animal) and to label and display their drawings on a bulletin board.

📖 *In the Woods: Who's Been Here?*

FICTION

by Lindsay Barrett George
New York: Greenwillow Books, 1995. 42p.

This large-format picture book has full-color, full-page illustrations. It will be enjoyed by primary-grade students.

As the story begins, William, Cammy, and their dog, Sam, set off for a walk in the woods on a cool and sunny autumn afternoon. When they reach an old cherry tree, they see an empty nest and wonder who has been here? On the next page, the question is answered. There is a picture of a northern oriole and its chicks in the nest.

When they see pinecone bits scattered on a stone, they wonder who has been *here*. A red squirrel. Then they wonder what left behind the chrysalis on a milkweed pod in a field. It was a monarch butterfly.

This format (seeing something, wondering about it, and then seeing a picture of the animal that has left its traces) is followed throughout the book. As the story continues, the children find indications that there have been recent visits by a snowshoe hare, a goshawk, a blue jay, a family of red foxes, a woodchuck, a mud dauber, and a deer.

Finally, the children come upon a tablecloth and basket and realize that their mother and father have come to the woods in time to share a picnic with them. A final page gives a paragraph of information about each of the animals that left traces in the woods.

Discussion Starters and Multidisciplinary Activities

1. Many animals in this book leave clues that they have visited a spot in the woods recently. Ask students which of the animal visitors is their favorite, and why.

2. Invite the students to describe something that they have seen in the woods, different from anything mentioned in this book, which was a clue that an animal had been visiting. Which animal was it?

3. Is there a favorite place in the woods, in a park, at the beach, or at a lake that students in the class enjoy visiting? Ask students to share their favorite places and tell why they enjoy visiting them.

4. The jacket flap map on the book shows a path that would make a good board game. Have students draw the map on a canvas board and divide the path into squares. Students go from start to finish by rolling a die and moving the number of spaces, *if* they can answer the question on the top card from a deck of cards. The cards can reflect any current topic being taught in class.

5. Acrostic poetry is fun to write. Students might choose a topic such as the woods. The first letter of each line, read from top to bottom, spells out the topic. For example:

Trees, green and still,	**W**ater, rippling in the creek,
Home to squirrels,	**O**wls, flying in the night.
Eyes of raccoons, staring,	**O**aks, bearing acorns,
	Deer, resting in the shade,
	Such a lovely place to visit!

6. Invite students to draw a picture of another woodland animal. Post these on the class bulletin board.

📖 *Mole's Hill: A Woodland Tale*

FICTION

by Lois Ehlert
San Diego: Harcourt Brace, 1994. 36p.

This large-format picture book has bright illustrations that were inspired by two art forms of the Woodland Indians, ribbon appliqué and sewn beadwork. There are both floral and geometric patterns. The book will be enjoyed by primary-grade readers.

When the story begins, it is dark in the wood and the stars are visible. But not everyone is sleeping. Fox is up and busy. Fox hears a scratching sound and realizes that mole is digging a tunnel. This irritates fox who believes that mole is always making a mess.

The next day when mole pops her head up from digging, she finds a note inviting her to meet fox, skunk, and raccoon that night at the maple tree. When the sun goes down, mole hurries to the meeting. Fox says that they are planning a path to the pond and that the mole hill is in the way and must go.

Raccoon explains that when the leaves turn colors, mole must move. Raccoon also reminds mole that fox has big teeth.

This news makes mole unhappy. She likes her home right where it is and she does not want to move. Mole gets an idea. A few days later when raccoon and skunk stroll by mole's hill, it is bigger than before. As many moons pass, the hill gets bigger and bigger. Then mole plants seeds on top of her big hill. Flowers and grass grow. When fall comes, and the animals look at the huge hill, fox asks mole to dig a tunnel so that their path can go through the hill. And that is exactly what mole does.

Discussion Starters and Multidisciplinary Activities

1 Fox seems to be a leader in this woodland animals group. Ask students to discuss why they think the other animals come to Fox's meetings and do whatever he asks.

2 When mole is told that she will have to move, she comes up with an idea. She builds an enormous hill. Have students discuss this plan and see if they can invent other ideas that might enable mole not to have to move.

3 Have students discuss why they think fox fell in with mole's alternative plan and did not demand that she move away.

4 Ask students to look at the two-page picture of the fox. It is not a realistic drawing, but is a picture made of geometric shapes. Have students make a drawing of any animal of their choice from triangles, squares, rectangles, circles, etc. Share the finished work.

5 The author says she wrote this story based on a fragment of a longer Native American legend. Ask a small group of students to prepare a list of other Native American legends available in the school library. Post this list of titles and authors in the classroom and encourage students to read some of these legends.

6 There may be someone in your community who is knowledgeable about Native American beadwork. Invite that person as a guest to share some beadwork. If possible, have the guest explain which American Indian tribes are famous for their beadwork and where they got their materials.

From *Exploring the World of Animals*. © 1997. Teacher Ideas Press. (800) 237-6124.

Prairie Dog Town

FICTION

by Bettye Rogers
Illustrated by Deborah Howland
Norwalk, CT: Soundprints, 1993. 32p.

This is one of a series of books in the Smithsonian Wild Heritage Collection on wildlife and habitats. The book alternates a page of text and a full-color illustration. It will be enjoyed by primary students.

As the story begins, a yearling prairie dog and his family enjoy the lushness of spring. But as summer comes and there is no rain, the prairie is baked dry, and the grasses shrivel and turn brown.

One morning when he wakes in his underground tunnel, prairie dog is hungry. He scurries up the tunnel and goes in search of food. He notices other heads popping out of the tunnels in prairie dog town. The animals greet each other by rubbing noses, and they groom one another's fur.

Although prairie dog eats some dry grass stems, digs roots, munches on prickly pear cactus, and finds some insects to eat, he is still hungry. When a hawk passes overhead, all the prairie dogs scurry back into their tunnels.

When the "all clear" is sounded, the prairie dogs come out of their tunnels and begin looking for food again. Each day food is harder to find, so prairie dog moves beyond the crowded town to a place where there is more food. Avoiding many dangers as he goes, prairie dog and other yearlings find an open, grassy stretch of prairie and begin to dig new burrows.

Discussion Starters and Multidisciplinary Activities

1 Ask students who have read the story to try to recall the different rooms that are described in prairie dog's burrow. Were they surprised to learn that a prairie dog's home is not just a tunnel but is made up of different rooms?

2 Ask students to discuss the feelings that prairie dog must have experienced as he left his home for the first time and traveled to a place for a new prairie dog town.

3 As prairie dog settles down to sleep in his new home for the first time, what might he be thinking and dreaming of? Encourage discussion.

4 Have the class display a prairie dog town on a bulletin board. In addition to the mounds of earth and the prairie dogs sticking their heads out of tunnels, pictures can include grasses, flowers, and butterflies, as well as other creatures, including burrowing owls, a hawk, a rattlesnake, a coyote, and a black-footed ferret.

5 Sometimes, because of disease or human construction, prairie dog towns are destroyed. The prairie dogs may be killed, or trapped and moved. With the help of a media specialist, see if two students can find newspaper or magazine reports of the destruction of a prairie dog town that they can share. Were the prairie dogs relocated or destroyed?

6 Invite a pair of students to research and share information about burrowing owls. How big are they? Where are they found? What do they eat? Why are they associated with prairie dogs?

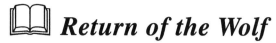

Return of the Wolf

by Dorothy Hinshaw Patent
Illustrated by Jared Taylor Williams
New York: Clarion Books, 1995. 67p.

F P272r

● **FICTION**

This unusual book is a story told from a wolf's point of view. A great deal of factual information about the habits and lifestyles of wolves is woven into the story. It will be enjoyed by readers in third through fifth grades.

Sedra, a young female wolf, is driven out of her pack because it is too large. She sets off alone to find where she can live and hunt. As she travels, she learns how difficult it is to catch and kill wild game when hunting alone, but she survives.

In another pack, a male wolf challenges the pack leader and loses. This defeated wolf, Jasper, is also forced to leave his pack and seek out a new home.

Jasper and Sedra meet, become friends, and hunt together. Sedra loses three of her toes to a steel trap, but recovers. Eventually they mate and have four pups named Raven, Ebony, Selina, and Tundra. The four wolves grow, face dangers, and begin to learn the skills of hunting.

During a hunt, a doe kicks Raven and Tundra. Afterwards, Tundra finds it very painful to breathe, but he eventually stands and is able to move. Raven, however, is dead. The wolves are forced to move on, their pack now reduced to five members, as they struggle to survive.

Discussion Starters and Multidisciplinary Activities

1   Ask students to discuss Sedra being caught in a trap. Did they think she would survive? Did they think a trapper might come and be part of the story?

2   The wolf pups are called Raven, Ebony, Selina, and Tundra. What would your students name the four wolf pups, and why?

3   The story opens with a wolf pack so large that Sedra is forced to leave. When the story ends, there are doubts if the five wolves can survive. Ask students to tell whether they think this little pack will thrive. Why?

4   Students can make a negative mold of an animal track by making a cardboard collar about 1-½ inches wide from a milk carton, finding an animal track left in a muddy place, and pushing the collar into the dirt or sand around the track. Fill the collar with a mixture of one cup water mixed with one cup plaster of paris. Let everything sit for thirty minutes. When the plaster is dry to the touch, peel away the cardboard. Lift up the negative mold of the track.

5   The author has studied wolves in Montana. Ask a small group of students to find out where most of the wolves in the United States and Canada currently live. In some places wolves have been reintroduced and then left alone in the wild. With the help of the media specialist, ask students to find and share a photocopy of a newspaper or magazine article on this topic.

6   Some states outlaw leg traps. Ask a pair of students to research current trapping practices. Does trapping go on in your state or neighboring states? What laws regulate trapping? What sorts of traps are allowed? What animals are commonly trapped?

 *The Spring Rabbit*

FICTION

by Joyce Dunbar
Illustrated by Susan Varley   *ED 911s*
New York: Lothrop, Lee & Shepard Books, 1994. 26p.

This picture book, illustrated with color drawings and containing only a few lines of text per page, will appeal to primary-grade readers.

The story is told by Smudge, a rabbit who is unhappy because he does not have any brothers or sisters. When Smudge complains about this to his mother, she tells him to wait until spring.

Spring seems a long time away to Smudge. In the autumn, he fashions a rabbit out of twigs and leaves and says it can be his brother. But the leafy rabbit cannot talk to Smudge or chase him down the hill. A wind comes up and blows the leafy rabbit away.

In the winter, Smudge makes a snow rabbit and says it can be his sister. But the snow rabbit cannot play with him either. And the next day, the snow rabbit melts.

After the snow melts, Smudge makes a mud rabbit to be his brother, but the mud rabbit cannot splash in puddles with him. Then the rain comes and washes the mud rabbit away.

When spring finally does come, Smudge looks everywhere for his brothers and sisters. He finds a mouse hole full of baby mice, a bird's nest with six speckled eggs, and tiny tadpoles in the pond. Discouraged, Smudge goes home, only to find that he now has two baby brothers and a baby sister. Spring has come.

Discussion Starters and Multidisciplinary Activities

1   Once Smudge has made a leafy rabbit that blows away in the wind, many students will be able to guess what Smudge will do when it snows. Invite students to predict what Smudge will do next and what might happen to each of the rabbits that he makes.

2   The other animals, such as the mouse and the bird, do not make fun of Smudge for creating rabbits out of leaves, snow, and mud. Each simply tells Smudge that he must wait until spring. Have students discuss why other animals are so kind to Smudge.

3   When spring comes, Smudge visits several places and sees babies. Invite students to suggest some other spots Smudge might have visited in the woods looking for baby rabbits and what kinds of babies he might have found.

4   If it snows in your part of the world, students have made snowmen. They might enjoy making a snow sculpture of a rabbit on a part of the school grounds. Some might make other animals such as a snow dragon. (If your area is not snowy, students might make their animals out of papier-mâché.)

5   A science experiment about melting could prove interesting. Freeze liquids such as water, orange juice, and soda pop into ice cubes. Have students predict which cubes will melt fastest, and why. Set out cubes and time how long they take to melt.

6   This book shows a frog pond full of tiny tadpoles. Ask a pair of interested students to research the growth of frogs and draw pictures showing each stage of their development until they are full-grown frogs.

FICTION

📖 *A Week of Raccoons*

by Gloria Whelan
Illustrated by Lynn Munsinger
New York: Alfred A. Knopf, 1988. 32p.

This picture book has amusing full-color illustrations and a simple text that will be enjoyed by primary-grade students.

Mr. and Mrs. Twerkle live in a little cottage next to a pond. One morning they discover that their potted petunias have been knocked over. Mr. Twerkle suspects a raccoon and decides to trap it and take it to the piny woods.

That night Mr. Twerkle sets his trap. The next morning he finds a raccoon in the cage. Mr. Twerkle puts the caged raccoon in his truck and drives by a tumble-down cabin, an apple tree, over a bridge, past a schoolhouse and farm, and then releases the raccoon in the piny woods.

On his return, Mr. Twerkle learns the hummingbird feeder has been knocked over. Thinking there is another raccoon, Mr. Twerkle sets his trap again. The next morning, he finds a second raccoon in the trap and drives to the piny woods and releases it.

The raccoons trapped on Monday and Tuesday meet in the piny woods and try to figure out how to return to the pond. Each remembers part of the way home. In the days that follow, raccoons continue to do mischief, get trapped, and are released in the piny woods. By putting together what they know, all five raccoons head home. But one decides to stay at the farm, one at the schoolhouse, one at the bridge, one at the apple tree, and one at the cabin. So Mr. and Mrs. Twerkle are left in peace.

Discussion Starters and Multidisciplinary Activities

1 From the title, students will suspect raccoons to be the mischief makers. Ask them to discuss what else might be the cause of the broken flower pots and the dug up petunias on the Twerkle's front porch.

2 Ask students if they thought more than one raccoon would be involved in the story. Why?

3 Ask students to guess whether Mr. and Mrs. Twerkle will be left in peace or whether some other animals will come to do mischief. Why?

4 Mr. Twerkle set a trap for raccoons. Interested students might set a beetle trap one night. Sink an empty coffee can in the earth so its rim is level with the ground. Drop in a piece of smelly meat, fish, or cheese. Put a small rock on either side of the can and a large, flat rock, resting on the small rocks, to cover the can and keep rain out. If you catch a beetle, be sure to let it go after you study it.

5 A group of students might want to write a sequel to this book. They could write and illustrate a picture book in which some other animal comes and causes problems for the Twerkles. Tell how the Twerkles solve this new problem. Allow time for students to share the sequel.

6 Raccoons look as if they are wearing masks. Invite students to draw the face of an animal large enough to fit them as a mask. Each student will draw, color, cut out, and wear a mask. Then students can guess what animal each classmate represents.

 *Wolf at the Door*

FICTION

by Barbara Corcoran
New York: Atheneum, 1993. 194p.

This contemporary story takes place in Wyoming and is told from the viewpoint of fourteen-year-old Lee McDougall. It will be enjoyed by fourth- and fifth-grade readers.

Lee McDougall, along with her mother, father, and sister, Savannah, have moved often. This time they are off to a new, woodsy cabin near Kalispell, Montana. On their drive to their new home, Lee and her mother find a neglected wolf in a roadside zoo. They later take the wolf, Ruthie, to their land. Lee plans to feature Ruthie in a picture book.

Lee's father settles into his new job at the radio station. Lee's mother hopes to get involved in a biological study at the university, and Savannah finds new friends and lots of activity in the local amateur theater company. Lee's grandmother, Savannah, is a famous aging actress, and it is generally assumed that young Savannah will follow in her grandmother's footsteps.

Many problems need to be worked out. A man who has heard reports about Ruthie comes and leaves four more wolves with Lee. Some of the ranchers are not pleased by wolves being kept nearby, and someone breaks the gate on their road and leaves an ugly message one night. Several men try to poison the wolves.

In the course of the book, Lee and Savannah come to appreciate each other. As the story ends, Savannah leaves to live and study with her grandmother, while Lee makes a long-term commitment to the wolves.

Discussion Starters and Multidisciplinary Activities

1 Did student's attitudes toward wolves change after reading this book? What do they think about wolves now? How did they view them before?

2 Savannah has just turned twelve. Do you think it is realistic that her parents would let her leave home and study with her grandmother? Why or why not?

3 As the story ends, both sisters are worried that the other will change. A year from the end of the story, do you think either of the sisters will have changed much?

4 In some parts of the country there have been efforts to restore wolves to areas from which they had been wiped out. With the help of a media specialist, ask a pair of students to try to locate articles that discuss reintroducing wolves. After their research the students should report what they have learned.

5 In the introduction to this book the author thanks Dorothy Patent for taking her to see a pack of wolves in northwestern Montana. Dorothy Patent is also an author who has written about wolves. Invite a student to research what books Dorothy Patent has written. If possible, the student should read and report on one of her books.

6 There are several groups devoted to defending wildlife. With the help of a media specialist, ask a pair of students to locate the names and addresses of some of these groups and write to *one* for information. Students should be sure to send a self-addressed, stamped envelope and share any material received.

Animals in the Woods

◆ *Bridges and Poetry* ◆

 Wild Voices

 *Winter's Orphans:
The Search for a
Family of Mountain
Lion Cubs*

*Birds, Beasts,
and Fishes:
A Selection of
Animal Poems*

 *Wild Voices*

BRIDGES AND POETRY

by Drew Nelson
Illustrated by John Schoenherr
New York: Philomel Books, 1991. 95p.

This "bridge" book is a series of short stories told from the point of view of the animals. There is no dialogue, but each short story has a plot and is filled with details about animal life. There are black-and-white sketches illustrating each chapter. It will appeal to third- through fifth-grade readers.

The book is divided into seven sections: Fox Trot, Missing Lynx, Roan, Puma, Lone Wolf, Nanny, and Patch. In Fox Trot, a hungry fox in February is unable to find enough food. She goes down to the farm and captures a hen. When she returns the next night the farm dog follows her. The fox manages to injure the dog's nose, but she must abandon her den and move to remain safe.

The lynx in the second chapter is not so lucky. It is caught in a leg trap and then killed by a hungry wolverine. The roan is successful in defending his harem of horses from a mustang who comes and challenges him. The roan is also successful in injuring the lead wolf and chasing off a pack of wolves who try to kill one of the foals.

Old and injured, the lead wolf is challenged by a young male who defeats him and drives him from the pack. The puma goes to the farm to kill a sheep and is shot by the farmer. The nanny goat delivers her kid in a snowstorm and successfully returns to the flock. In the final story, Patch, an old and faithful dog, is shot by its master to put it out of its misery.

Possible Topics for Further Investigation

1   All of the animals in this book leave distinct tracks in the snow and mud. People who study tracks can recognize the animal from the tracks that it leaves. Bring to class some books showing animal tracks. Have students choose a favorite track, draw it on a piece of paper, and cut it out. Cut a potato in half. Give half of a potato to each student. Each student will trace a track on the cut piece of potato. Then, carefully using a knife,* cut or scrape away the potato surface, leaving the print sticking up. Each student can dip the potato into poster paint and then make prints on paper to make a greeting card or to be used as wrapping paper.

2   Animals follow paths and trails. Students also travel paths to reach school, visit a friend's house, etc. This would be a good time to teach mapping skills. Ask each student to make a map showing a frequently used route. Have the students label street or road names, major landmarks, etc. Allow time for students to share and explain their maps.

3   Most states have adopted a state animal. It may be a common animal or even an endangered species. Have a pair of students research your state animal. Have them draw a picture of this animal and write a report about the animal and when it was chosen to be a state symbol. If your state has adopted a state bird, fish, tree, flower, or other symbol, have students include that information in their report too. Allow time for students to share what they learn.

* Review with children all safety precautions about using knives before letting them do this!

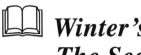

Winter's Orphans: The Search for a Family of Mountain Lion Cubs

by Robert C. Farentinos
Illustrated by Shannon Keegan
Niwot, CO: Roberts Rinehart Publishers, 1993. 64p.

This book was selected as a "bridge" book because it is a true story with fictional elements of suspense and adventure. The author describes in first person how he helped find and raise the orphan cubs of a mountain lion that was shot near his home in Colorado. Part of the book is a "dream sequence" told from the point of view of one of the lion cubs. This book is illustrated with both color and black-and-white drawings and will be enjoyed by students in grades three through five.

An angry resident in the mountains of Colorado shoots and kills a mountain lion that he sees pursuing chickens and geese near his mountain home. A neighbor, a wildlife biologist with a different attitude toward mountain lions, begins the almost impossible task of finding the mountain lion's orphan cubs.

The biologist finds the four cubs and watches them unobserved. He names the largest cub, Lanthito, the unseen one. After his first encounter, days pass without the cubs being spotted again. One of the cubs is run down by a car on the canyon road and killed. Finally, the biologist captures Lanthito, and then the two sister cubs by using baited traps. He takes them home and helps transfer them to a rehabilitation center where they live until they are strong enough to be released again into their natural habitat.

Possible Topics for Further Investigation

1   Two points of view are described in this book. From one viewpoint, the mountain lion is a dangerous animal that kills livestock and dogs and poses a threat to the people who live in the mountains. These people feel comfortable in killing mountain lions. Others, like the wildlife biologist, believe there must be a better way of dealing with the clash between humans and mountain lions sharing the same area. Students might want to invite someone from the state's wildlife division to discuss this topic.

2   The artist uses black-and-white sketches throughout the nonfiction portion of this book and uses color drawings during the dream sequence when the cub tells his story. Invite interested students to choose a section from the book to illustrate. They may use any media and work in black-and-white or in color. Share the results with the class by including the drawings on a class bulletin board.

3   A small group of students may want to research prehistoric cats. Cats can be traced back forty million years and were descendants of early meat eaters, called *Miacids*. The first true cat was a North American animal called *Dinictis*. The cat family eventually split into two branches, the *Felidae,* or biting cats, and the *Machairodontinae,* or stabbing cats, like the sabertooths. Once students have completed their research, ask them to share a little of the ancestry of cats with class members.

BRIDGES AND POETRY

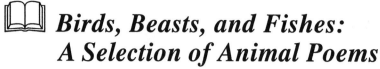

📖 *Birds, Beasts, and Fishes: A Selection of Animal Poems*

selected by Anne Carter
Illustrated by Reg Cartwright
New York: Macmillan, 1991. 64p.

808.1
C245b

This large-format book contains a collection of poetry with vivid color illustrations on every page. The poems will appeal to students in kindergarten through fifth grade.

The book begins with poems about birds. Among the poems included are: The Eagle, The Vulture, Pigeon and Wren, The Cormorant, The Pelican Chorus, The Twa Corbies, Sweet Suffolk Owl, Captive Bird, The Windhover, The Owl, and Night Heron.

The next section has poems about other flying creatures entitled: The Wasp, The Bat, and Flying Crooked. Then there are poems about miscellaneous animals such as The Tiger, Upon the Snail, The Poor Man's Pig, Worms and the Wind, The Rabbit, On a Cat Aging, Cat at the Cream, The Cat's Song, Camels of the Kings, Hares at Play, The Vixen, First Sight, The Jaguar, The Gazelle Calf, The Pied Piper of Hamelin, Two Performing Elephants, The Duck and the Kangaroo, Lizard, The Cow, The Ass in the Lion's Skin, The Flower Fed Buffaloes, Buffalo Dusk, A Prayer to Go to Paradise with the Donkeys, Pike, The Walrus, The Waterbeetle, The Octopus, Fish Riddle, Tidings, and The Fish.

Some of the poems are very short and others are long; many are humorous, while some are sad and mysterious. Authors of some poems are anonymous, while others are quite famous.

Discussion Starters and Multidisciplinary Activities

1. Ask students to read the two poems about cats on page 31. Have them write down unknown words and guess their meaning to make sense of the poems. Then have the students look up the following words in the glossary: een and thrum. With this help, can they figure out the meaning of the poems?

2. Invite students to read the bird poems on pages 6 through 20. Have them discuss their favorite one and explain why they like it best.

3. Read and discuss with students "First Sight," by Philip Larkin on page 36. The poet describes snow as a "vast unwelcome" and a "sunless glare." But as the lamb waits by the ewe, something else is waiting in surprise. What is it that will "wake and grow utterly unlike the snow?"

4. The poem on page 40 is just a selection from a longer poem, "The Pied Piper of Hamelin." Have a pair of interested students find a copy of the entire poem by Robert Browning, and share it with the class.

5. Ogden Nash wrote the four-line poem, "The Octopus," on page 55. He uses end rhyme and humor. Invite interested students to write their own four-line humorous poems about animals of their choice. Take time to share these.

6. There are a lot of unusual words in "The Poor Man's Pig." Ask students to write out definitions for the following: knarred, ere, osiers, sow, orts, pullets, and sulky.

Animals in the Woods

Nonfiction Connections

Amazing Bears

by Theresa Greenaway
New York: Alfred Knopf, 1992. 32p.

**NONFICTION
CONNECTIONS**

This book is part of the Eyewitness Juniors series focusing on living animals and working machines. *Amazing Bears* has several two-page sections on a variety of bears. It is illustrated with color photographs and will appeal to readers in grades two through five.

The book begins by answering the question, "What is a bear?" This section describes the jaws, paws, and senses of bears, as well as differentiates bears, which are mammals, from koalas, which are marsupials.

The section on the American black bear explains that it is the most common bear in North America with an estimated 750,000 black bears living in Canada, the United States, and Mexico.

Sun bears, also called Malayan and honey bears, are the smallest of all bears. They live in Southeast Asia. Polar bears live in the frozen sea around the North Pole and eat more meat than other bears. The 2,000 spectacled bears that have survived are found in the tropical forest of the northern Andes mountains in South America.

There are brown bears in Europe, North America, and Asia. North American brown bears are called grizzlies because some of them have fur tipped with silver white. The Kodiak bear in Alaska is the largest brown bear. Sloth bears live in India, Nepal, and Sri Lanka. The Asiatic black bear is found in eastern Asia and Japan, while the giant panda lives in western China.

Possible Topics for Further Investigation

1   Experts argue about whether the red panda is a panda or a raccoon. A media specialist might help a pair of students research the red panda. Are there scientific journals or magazines that have reported on the topic? Do most experts favor including it with raccoons or with panda bears? Why? Ask the students to report what they learn and describe their research techniques and sources used.

2   Many bears are favorites in stories for children. One of the most loved is "Winnie the Pooh" along with his friends, Piglet, Eeyore, Owl, Tigger, and Rabbit. A small group of interested students might choose a section from one of the Pooh books for dramatization. Using a narrator, the actors could stage one of Pooh's adventures and present it to a class of kindergarten students. They will need simple costumes and props and time for rehearsal.

3   Yellowstone National Park was once very famous for its bears. Visitors who go to the park now, seldom see a bear. Ask a group of interested students to research Yellowstone bears. What are some of the problems that they caused? What solutions were found for these problems? Why do the bears seem scarce in the park now? What are wise rules with respect to bears that visitors should follow? A letter requesting information to the Park Headquarters, which includes a self-addressed, stamped envelope, may provide useful information.

 *Busy Beavers*

by M. Barbara Brownell

Washington, DC: National Geographic Society, 1988. 34p.

This book is one of a series produced by the National Geographic Society called Books for Young Explorers. It is a large-format book with simple text and full-color photographs and will appeal to readers in grades two through four.

This book explains how beavers eat grass and weeds beside their pond and how they build their homes. They first use sticks to dam up water to make a pool, and then gnaw down small trees to make their homes, or lodges, that they build out in the deep water. In addition to branches, beavers use mud and old grass from the bottom of the pond and pack them into cracks to get the lodge ready for winter. The entrance to the lodge is under water, but there is also a dry shelf above water inside the lodge.

Because they cannot run fast, beavers stay near the water. They dig canals from the woods back down to their pond. If the beaver senses danger, it hurries to the water and slaps its broad, flat tail to warn other beavers of nearby danger.

Special adaptations of the beaver's body are explained. Its teeth have a hard, orange coating which helps prevent them from chipping. Its hind feet are webbed like a duck's, which help it swim very fast. A layer of fat keeps it warm and its fur is thick and waterproof. Clear lids, under the eyelids, close when the beaver is underwater, and it can see right through them.

Females usually have four or more babies, or kits, which nurse and eventually also eat grass, twigs, and bark.

Possible Topics for Further Investigation

1. Students might enjoy writing and illustrating a picture book to share with a kindergarten class. Each student could choose an animal, draw its picture, and write the text for one page of the book. It could be a book about animal expressions including such phrases as "busy as a beaver," "hungry as a bear," "quiet as a mouse," etc. The whole class might brainstorm a list of these expressions, and then each student could choose one from the list to include in the book.

2. Beavers belong to the animal order *Rodentia*. These are animals that gnaw and include squirrels, mice, rats, and others. There are more rodents than any other order of mammals. Invite a pair of students to research rodents. They might make a list of as many rodents as they can, as well as other interesting facts about some members of the rodent family. When the two students are ready, have them share their information.

3. Around the year 1900 beavers were almost extinct. They had been killed off in huge numbers for their fur. Ask a group of interested students to learn more about the beaver fur trade in North America and report back to class. How did the fur trappers go about their business? Where were most of the beavers trapped? How did the trappers get their furs to market? What companies traded and paid for furs? Where were most of the beaver furs sold and what were they used for? When did the beaver fur trading end, and what were the causes that led it to stop?

I See Animals Hiding

by Jim Arnosky
New York: Scholastic, 1995. 28p.

NONFICTION
CONNECTIONS

This picture book tells about shy, wild animals that hide in the woods. The illustrations are softly colored with animals blending in with their surroundings. It will be enjoyed by primary-grade readers.

The book begins by showing a porcupine hiding in a tree. The text explains that because there are many dangers to animals in the wild, they are shy and always hiding. Two woodcocks are shown on the leafy ground. Their protective coloration, called camouflage, allows them to blend with their surroundings. Three deer are partially hidden when they lie down among tall grasses and small shrubby trees in the meadow. A two-page spread in the book invites the reader to find all twenty deer on a snowy hill. The deer have shed their summer coats for grayer winter coats that blend better with the leafless trees.

The snowshoe hare also changes the color of its coat from brown to winter white and becomes almost invisible in snow. Other white animals, hard to see in the snow, are the arctic fox, long-tailed weasel, and the snowy owl.

The screech owl blends in perfectly with the gray coloring of the tree bark where it perches. A moth, the same color as the bark, is also hiding on the tree. Speckled trout swim among speckled stones in the water. A garter snake looks like a broken branch on the ground. A bittern blends in with reeds and cattails, and a raccoon hides in a hollow log.

Possible Topics for Further Investigation

1   One of the birds featured in this book is a bittern. It will be familiar to some students but not to others. Invite a small group of students to research this bird. What is its size? What is its range? Where does it winter? What is its habitat? What does it eat? What kind of song or call does it make? What herons are closely related to the bittern? The students should share what they learn.

2   If you share this book with the art specialist in your school, it might become the basis for an interesting art lesson. Each student could sketch and color a woodland creature camouflaged in its natural environment. The completed drawings could be labeled and hung on a bulletin board.

3   Some students like to make and solve word searches or crossword puzzles. Invite pairs of students who are interested to make a word search or a crossword puzzle. Graphing paper is useful for this project. Remind students that in a word search you might find the word horizontally, vertically, or diagonally. For the crossword puzzle, students need to identify whether the words are "across" or "down" and need to supply clues to aid in solving the puzzle. Several of the camouflaged creatures from I See Animals Hiding should be included in these word games. When the word searches and crossword puzzles are completed, have them duplicated so that other students in the class may try to solve them.

📖 # *The Case of Mummified Pigs: And Other Mysteries in Nature*

NONFICTION
CONNECTIONS

by Susan E. Quinlan

Honesdale, PA: Boyds Mills Press, 1995. 128p.

This book, illustrated with black-and-white sketches, will interest students in grades three through five. It contains fourteen sections or mysteries on such varied topics as butterflies, hares, mummified pigs, mice, ants, and peregrines. The book was written by a wildlife biologist who follows scientists as they track clues about scientific mysteries and the way nature works.

The sections of greatest interest for students studying wild mammals are "The Mystery of Saint Matthew Island," "The Mystery of the Disappearing Hares," "The Puzzle in the Postcard Scene," "The Case of the Mummified Pigs," and "The Case of the Twin Islands."

Saint Matthew Island boasted a herd of six thousand reindeer, but in 1965 the herd was down to only forty-two animals. The clue to what had happened was discovered in their skeletons.

Another scientific puzzle surrounds populations of snowshoe hares, which surge in ten-year cycles in the northern woods. Many suggestions, put forward by a scientist named Bryant, concluded that new shoots of plants, which the hares commonly ate, contained a concentration of chemicals poisonous to the hares.

In each of the mysteries explored in this book, students will have an opportunity to see how scientists come up with and test explanations for scientific mysteries.

Possible Topics for Further Investigation

1 The science mysteries in this book occur in various parts of the world. Ask a pair of students to list the book's scientific mysteries on a sheet of paper and label each mystery 1, 2, 3, etc. Place the list next to a map of the world on the class bulletin board. Have students insert a pin with corresponding flags labeled 1, 2, 3, etc., to show where each of these scientific mysteries took place. For example, the first mystery in the book is "The Mystery of Saint Matthew Island." Find Saint Matthew Island in the Bering Sea and insert a pin with a flag labeled "#1."

2 What was learned in the experiment with the mummified pigs sheds light on why mummies were prepared in special ways in Egypt before being stored in tombs. Ask a small group of students to learn and report what they can find out about a specific Egyptian tomb and mummies. Have these students share what they learn.

3 "The Mice, the Ants, and the Desert Plants" pointed out that although ants do not eat mice, and mice do not eat ants, the number of mice affects the number of ants. Ask a pair of interested students to prepare a large wall chart explaining how the life and health of mice, ants, and desert plants interact. When their research and chart is complete, ask the two students to explain the interactive process to the rest of the class.

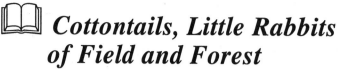

Cottontails, Little Rabbits of Field and Forest

NONFICTION CONNECTIONS

by Ron Fisher

Washington, DC: The National Geographic Society, 1989. 34p.

This large-format book will be enjoyed by second- and third-grade readers. Kindergarten pupils and first graders will also enjoy the full-color photographs. There is minimal text, but the book includes two packed pages of information for teachers in the back, as well as a list of books that might be of interest for additional reading.

The book points out that there are fourteen kinds of cottontails, each with a different name. The first animal shown is a desert cottontail. This is followed by the eastern cottontail and a mountain cottontail. Vocabulary is developed as the reader learns that the babies are called kittens, kittens old enough to leave the nest are called juveniles, the mother rabbits are called does, and the father rabbits are called bucks.

Other wild rabbits pictured in the book are the marsh rabbit, ryukyu rabbit, Bushman hare, hispid hare, volcano rabbit, European rabbit, and red rock rabbit.

There is a short section on domestic rabbits including: broken tortoise English lop, black harlequin, black English spot, Belgian hare, blue rex, Florida white, black Dutch, black checkered giant, solid steel French lop, white English angora, dwarf hotot, and broken agouti mini lop.

The book describes how these rabbits eat, dig a shallow resting place called a "form," "freeze," wash themselves, and care for their young.

Possible Topics for Further Investigation

1 Show students the pictures of the rabbits and tracks in the snow that appear on pages 12 and 13. Discuss with them what it might be that caused the rabbit to run away. There may be many suggestions, ranging from a person or dog, to a big mountain lion. Have each student write a short story about the incident. When the stories are complete, plan a story time when those who are willing to read their rabbit adventure stories aloud can do so. Encourage students to make an illustration.

2 If there is someone in your immediate area that raises rabbits, invite that person to come to class and talk about the care of rabbits. If possible, the visitor might bring a rabbit along that the children could see and pet. Be sure that children are comfortable with the rabbit and that they know how to safely handle one without frightening it or being rough. Follow up the visit with a thank-you note.

3 Pikas, rabbits, and hares are all members of the order of mammals called *Lagomorpha*. They have many enemies. Ask a small group of students to prepare a bulletin board about the *Lagomorphs*. They could make a woodland scene with life-sized drawings of several kinds of rabbits and include drawings of their many ground enemies including foxes, weasels, bobcats, coyotes, snakes, dogs, and badgers, as well as eagles, hawks, and owls, which hunt them from the sky. Ask the students to label each of their drawings.

Playful Slider, The North American River Otter

by Barbara Juster Esbensen
Illustrated by Mary Barrett Brown
Boston: Little, Brown, 1993. 32p.

NONFICTION CONNECTIONS

This picture book is illustrated with color drawings and will be enjoyed by second- through fourth-grade readers.

While most mammals play only when they are young, river otters, who may live to reach twenty years of age, remain playful throughout their lives. This makes them quite different from their other relatives that belong to the *Mustelidae,* or weasel family, such as the badger, skunk, and wolverine.

This book begins by showing a pair of otters sliding down from the top of a snowy hill. Then the otters begin a lively game of hide and seek in which one pops its head up and then disappears into the snow to be chased by the other.

The otter is long and slender with a rich, brown fur. It has a wide, flat head and a short muzzle. Although it can run on land, its streamlined body makes the otter a powerful underwater swimmer. The otter's main food is fish. Otters live in dens near the water and dig a tunnel so that one entrance to the den is under water. In winter, they swim under the ice searching for food. They also eat insects, snakes, and snails. The young are born in the spring and the mother provides them milk. They are helpless at first and do not come out of the den until they are three months old. Then they learn to swim and catch fish. The young otters remain with their mother through the winter until the following spring.

Possible Topics for Further Investigation

1 This book explains that otters belong to the *Mustelidae,* or weasel family. Ask a group of seven students to prepare a class bulletin board on the *Mustelidae.* Each student will find or draw a picture and write a one-page report on one of the following family members: otter, skunk, fisher, badger, marten, wolverine, or mink. In their reports, students should describe how big the animal is, what it eats, who its enemies are, and where it can be found.

2 In spring, summer, autumn, and winter, otters are busily engaged in many activities. Four students might work together to draw each season, featuring the activities of otters. For example, in spring the baby otters may be with their mother in the den. In summer the otters could be swimming or catching food near the bottom of the river. In autumn they could be playing on a river bank beneath red and gold fall leaves. In winter the otters could be sliding across the snow. Students may use whatever media they most enjoy, and the four pictures could be displayed in the classroom.

3 The river otter has another interesting relative that is not discussed in this book, the sea otter. The sea otter (*Enhydra lutris*) is the only living marine species of this group of animals. Sea otters range along the coast of the Bering Sea and the Pacific Ocean. Ask a pair of students to learn and report about sea otters including: their size, what they eat, where they are found, and how they raise their young.

Meet the Moose

by Leonard Lee Rue III
with William Owen
New York: Dodd, Mead, 1985. 78p.

This book, illustrated with black-and-white photographs, will be enjoyed by fourth- and fifth-grade readers.

Meet the Moose is divided into eight chapters: "Meet the Moose," "Moose Antlers," "Range Today," "Eating Habits," "From Birth to Old Age," "Moose in Winter," "Moose Enemies," and "Moose and People." There is also an index.

Few people see moose in the wild and so they do not appreciate how large the moose is. Males can stand seven feet tall at the shoulder and weigh 1,400 pounds. Because they are so large, they need a great deal of food. Moose eat only plants and they consume about fifty pounds of food day. They are black, dark brown, or russet.

For animals as large as moose, they can move amazingly fast. They have very long legs, which helps them both when they browse in a creek and when they must move through the deep snow.

The antlers of a male moose are six feet across on average and weigh about sixty pounds. The antlers are palmate with prongs projecting up like fingers. Both males and females have a bell or pendant hanging down beneath the throat. Babies are born in late May or early June and weigh about thirty pounds at birth.

Moose are found in the forested parts of northern United States and in Canada. They also live in Alaska, Nova Scotia, and Newfoundland.

Possible Topics for Further Investigation

1. An animal as large as a moose would appear to have few enemies, and this is generally true. Yet moose are sometimes attacked and killed by other animals. Invite a pair of students to research moose enemies. How can wolves, for example, kill a huge moose? How are young moose calves sometimes killed by predators? Is there danger from wolverines, cougars, black bears, or grizzly bears? What is the moose's greatest natural killer? Have these students report what they learn.

2. This book gives factual information about moose. Ask a small group of students to use the data presented here to prepare an interesting set of math problems for their classmates to solve. Have the students write the problems (and their answers) and then prepare a work sheet to distribute to other students. Problems might include: If a moose eats fifty pounds of food a day in winter, how many days would it take for one moose to eat a ton of food? If a moose eats sixty pounds of food a day in summer, how many pounds would a moose eat from July 1 through September 30?

3. Ticks are a problem for moose. A moose may have hundreds of ticks on its body. In some parts of the country, people also gets ticks. If you live in an area where ticks are a problem, invite an expert to come to class and discuss ticks. What are they? Why are they dangerous? How can you avoid getting ticks? What do you do if a tick embeds itself in you?

Wolves

by Seymour Simon
New York: HarperCollins, 1993. 32p.

599.742
Si 55w

This book is illustrated with full-page, full-color remarkable photographs and will be enjoyed by students in grade three through five. The text suggests that readers who learn more about wolves and how they live will be able to tell the differences between the real animals and the legends and fables in which wolves are often depicted as treacherous, sly, and evil.

The author points out that in many ways, wolves are like dogs and lions. Yet while people call dogs their best friends, and admire lions, they often dislike wolves and fail to recognize that wolves tend to be loyal, friendly, playful, and intelligent.

Information is provided about the parts of the world where wolves can live, their diet, size, and types of coats. Close relatives are the domestic dog, the coyote, the jackal, and Australia's dingo. Although there are different kinds of wolves, all belong to the same species called *Canis lupus.*

The book provides considerable information. Wolves are the largest members of the dog family and an adult can weigh from 40 to 175 pounds and stretch more than six feet from the tip of the nose to the end of its tail. They have powerful jaws and pointed teeth and are well suited for catching and eating animals. Many wolves live in packs. Litters are born usually in May, in dens where the pups grow rapidly and are ready to join the pack in the fall. Only small numbers of wolves still survive throughout the world.

Possible Topics for Further Investigation

1. This book explains the different kinds of teeth that a wolf has and the special functions of canines, incisors, and carnassials. Ask a pair of students to find out about human teeth. They will want to set up an interview with a local dentist. An adult needs to be available to provide transportation to and from the interview. Using a drawing, ask the students to make a presentation to the class sharing their research by showing and naming the types of teeth in the human mouth and telling about their special functions.

2. Like bats and dolphins, wolves can hear high-pitched sounds. Let six students work in pairs to learn more about the special hearing abilities of wolves, bats, and dolphins. When they have completed their research, ask the students to make a presentation to the class sharing what they have learned.

3. Using just the material provided in this book, ask a pair of interested students to prepare a set of six math problems for the class to solve. Examples include: If there are 20 wolves in the pack, and each wolf eats 15 pounds of meat, how much meat will be left from an adult moose which had 1000 pounds of edible meat? If ten wolves weighed the following (56 pounds, 135 pounds, 73 pounds, 91 pounds, 81 pounds, 58 pounds, 97 pounds, 105 pounds, 62 pounds, 122 pounds), what is the average weight of the wolves?

From *Exploring the World of Animals.* © 1997. Teacher Ideas Press. (800) 237-6124.

📖 *The Wonder of Wolves*

adapted by Patricia Lantier-Sampon
from Tom Wolpert's *Wolf Magic for Kids*
Milwaukee: Gareth Stevens, 1992. 48p.

This book has large print with about thirty words to a page and is illustrated with full-page color photographs. It will appeal to readers in first and second grades.

The text explains that wolves are ancestors of dogs and that the gray wolf of North America looks a lot like a German shepherd. In addition to gray, wolves are also sometimes black, golden brown, rusty red, and even white.

In simple terms, the text explains that the different coloration of wolves helps them to blend in with their surroundings. The dark coat of the timber wolf helps hide it in the forest, while tundra wolves have white fur blending in with the snowy areas where they live.

Wolves mate in late winter, and the mother digs a den in a dry spot close to a water supply. The baby wolves are called pups. They are part of a group of wolves called a pack. All the wolves in a pack obey the leader.

Wolves are great hunters, searching for game over a large territory. They may trot as far as forty miles in search of food without stopping to rest. They use their keen sense of smell to follow the trail of their prey. After a kill, the leader eats first, before the rest of the wolves in the pack.

Wolves "speak" to each other by making sounds that appear to have special meaning to the other wolves.

Possible Topics for Further Investigation

1 This book briefly talks about the timber wolf, the gray wolf, and the tundra wolf. With the help of an adult volunteer, have a small group of students do library research on each of these three kinds of wolves. The adult can help the young students organize what they learn into a large chart giving the same type of information about each of the wolves. Categories might include: name, size, place(s) where it lives, coloration, typical diet, etc. When students have finished their research, post their chart in the classroom.

2 Encourage a group of interested students to prepare habitat scenes as shoebox dioramas. The habitat of the grey wolf, tundra wolf, and timber wolf can each be depicted in a different shoebox setting. Small plastic animals could be used or students could use paper cutouts. Real dirt, rocks, and twigs could be used to create each wolf setting. Cut paper and colored drawings could be used for a backdrop. Display these dioramas, with labels, in the classroom or media center.

3 Many students will have heard stories such as *Red Riding Hood* in which the wolf is the villain. This book encourages students to look at wolves in another way. With an adult volunteer, have a small group of students write an original story in which a wolf plays an important part. Record the story with different student voices for each part. Then have the students make simple puppets and present an original puppet show.

📖 *Wonders of Foxes*

by Sigmund A. Lavine
New York: Dodd, Mead, 1986. 80p.

NONFICTION
CONNECTIONS

This book is illustrated with black-and-white drawings and photographs and will be enjoyed by fourth- and fifth-grade readers.

Wonders of Foxes is divided into six chapters, "Meet the Fox," "Lore of the Fox," "Physical Characteristics," "Ways of the Fox," "A Skulk of Foxes," and "Man and the Red Fox." There is also an index.

Foxes, which are doglike animals, first appeared on earth about 40 million years ago. They are members of the family *Canidae*. Experts currently recognize twenty-one living species of fox. Most of the information in this book concerns the common red fox, which is the most widely distributed of all the foxes.

There are many stories and superstitions regarding the fox, and, in many societies, the fox has been considered to be evil.

The average red fox measures between two to three feet long from the tip of its nose to the tip of its tail. Its long fur makes it look larger than it really is. Foxes trot at about five miles an hour. They eat almost anything, including eggs, field mice, frogs, lizards, ground squirrels, and birds.

Short sections are devoted to a discussion of the gray fox, swift fox, kit fox, arctic fox, bat-eared fox, fennec, crab-eating fox, and other foxlike animals. The book concludes with a discussion of man's mixed feelings toward the red fox.

Possible Topics for Further Investigation

1 Paleontologists have established that foxes first appeared on earth during the period of time called the *Oligocene*, about 40 million years ago. Have a pair of students make a chart showing the major divisions of geologic time and the number of years covered in each period. The students should be sure to include the *Oligocene* on their chart so that classmates will recognize that this was a comparatively short time ago.

2 On page 15, a short statement informs the reader that the Apache revered the fox for sticking its tail into a flame tended by the gods and stealing fire for mankind. Invite a small group of students to work together to write and illustrate a picture book around this theme. One or more of the students may write the story and divide it to fit into a twenty-eight page format. Then one or more students may edit the book and prepare it for illustration by entering the text into a word processing program and printing it. Another pair of students could illustrate the book. Finally, a student might be willing to share the completed picture book with another class.

3 One of the animals shown in this book is the arctic fox, which has two color phases. One is a brown summer coat and the other a white winter coat. Have a pair of students research what other animals in snow country have two seasonal colors. Ask these students to find pictures and share the information about these animals.

The World of Squirrels

NONFICTION
CONNECTIONS

by Jennifer Coldrey
Milwaukee: Gareth Stevens Children's Books, 1986. 32p.

This book has a simple text and is illustrated with color photographs supplied by Oxford Scientific Films. It will be enjoyed by second- and third-grade readers.

First, the text explains that there are many kinds of squirrels and that they live in habitats that include parks, yards, and forests in North America, Europe, Africa, and Asia. All of them, however, make trees their home.

Trees provide most of the squirrel's food, including nuts, seeds, buds and shoots, and fruits. Sometimes squirrels bury nuts and pinecones to eat at a future time. They build hollow nests, called dreys, in trees. The dreys are built of twigs and bark and then lined with moss, grass, and leaves.

Tree squirrels come in many colors, including grey, brown, and red. They have long bushy tails and sleek fur. They use their tails to steer and balance in trees. Some types of squirrels have tufts of hair on their ears.

Squirrels have good eyesight, hearing, and sense of smell. Like all members of the rodent family, squirrels have long, sharp front teeth called incisors, which they use for gnawing and cutting. They also have grinding teeth called molars.

Squirrels have babies once or twice a year. A baby squirrel weighs only one-half ounce and is 4 inches long, including its tail. The mother keeps the babies warm and feeds them milk.

Possible Topics for Further Investigation

1 Ask a small group of students to prepare a section of a bulletin board titled "Enemies of Squirrels." In the center of the bulletin board there should be a tree with branches and a nest of baby squirrels. An adult squirrel should be pictured on the ground. Enemies might include a bird of prey at the nest, a weasel or martin climbing the tree to attack the babies, snakes, dogs, or foxes that may attack the squirrel on the ground.

2 Squirrels can be pests. They chew telephone lines, eat holes in wooden and plastic bird feeders, peel rings of bark off of trees and kill them, and run off with pieces of doormats and mops to line their nests. Have a pair of students write and illustrate a humorous picture book in which a squirrel, or a family of squirrels, annoy some people. Have the people who are being pestered come up with an interesting way of dealing with the pesky squirrel(s) without causing injury. Allow time for the students to share their finished book with a kindergarten class.

3 When we think of nests in trees, we usually think of birds. But squirrels and many other animals also make nests in trees. Ask a small group of students to do library research with the help of the school media specialist or an adult volunteer. What other animals besides birds and squirrels make nests in trees? Have the students clip or photocopy pictures of these other nest builders and share their information.

Part IV
Animals in the Wild

Clare Miller

Animals in the Wild

● FICTION ●

- 📖 *The Boy Who Spoke Chimp*
- 📖 *A Camel Called April*
- 📖 *Crocodile! Crocodile! Stories Told Around the World*
- 📖 *The Elephant in the Dark*
- 📖 *The Great American Elephant Chase*

- 📖 *Jaguarundi*
- 📖 *Kalinzu, A Story from Africa*
- 📖 *Mary's Tiger*
- 📖 *Nanta's Search for Lion*
- 📖 *Sungura and Leopard, A Swahili Trickster Tale*
- 📖 *The Talking Earth*

◆ BRIDGES AND POETRY ◆

- 📖 *Legs: The Story of a Giraffe*
- 📖 *When Hippo Was Hairy, and Other Tales from Africa*
- 📖 *Wild Critters*

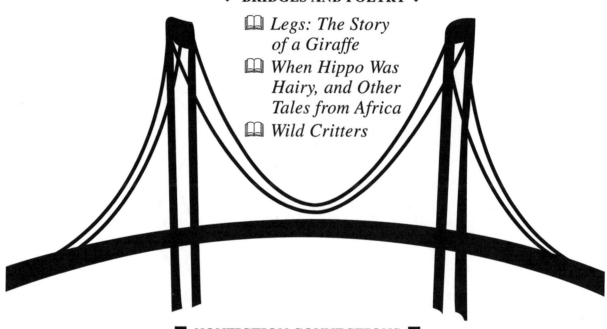

■ NONFICTION CONNECTIONS ■

- 📖 *Africa's Animal Giants*
- 📖 *Arctic Tundra*
- 📖 *The Caribou*
- 📖 *Endangered Animal Babies*
- 📖 *The Endangered Florida Panther*
- 📖 *Endangered Savannah Animals*

- 📖 *Kangaroos on Location*
- 📖 *Lion*
- 📖 *Primates: Lemurs, Monkeys, and You*
- 📖 *Tiger, Tiger, Growing Up*
- 📖 *To the Top of the World, Adventures with Arctic Wolves*

—OTHER TOPICS TO EXPLORE—

—acid rain	—extinction	—rain forests	—wart hogs
—cheetahs	—jackals	—sloths	—water buffalo
—endangered species list	—oxpeckers	—tropical hardwoods	—wild animal parks

---

From *Exploring the World of Animals*. © 1997. Teacher Ideas Press. (800) 237-6124.

● *Fiction* ●

- 📖 *The Boy Who Spoke Chimp*
- 📖 *A Camel Called April*
- 📖 *Crocodile! Crocodile! Stories Told Around the World*
- 📖 *The Elephant in the Dark*
- 📖 *The Great American Elephant Chase*
- 📖 *Jaguarundi*
- 📖 *Kalinzu, A Story from Africa*
- 📖 *Mary's Tiger*
- 📖 *Nanta's Search for Lion*
- 📖 *Sungura and Leopard, A Swahili Trickster Tale*
- 📖 *The Talking Earth*

The Boy Who Spoke Chimp

FICTION

by Jane Yolen
Illustrated by David Wiesner
New York: Alfred A. Knopf, 1981. 120p.

This story, set in California, is told in the third person by a twelve-year-old boy named Kriss. It will be enjoyed by third- and fourth-grade readers.

Kriss is hopeless in the woods, so his parents are sending him to camp in his grandmother's backyard near Big Sur. Planning to ride as far as Soledad and then hike the rest of the way on his own, Kriss leaves early and alone for the bus station. He does not have enough money to ride the bus, so he hitches rides and make it to Route 1, running along the coastline, where he is picked up by a driver in a white van.

The van contains chimps from the UCLA Language Lab that can talk in sign language. A radio warns that an earthquake is predicted, but Ed, the van driver, says it will only be a little tremor. An enormous earthquake hits, cars are overturned, and the road becomes a mass of tumbled blocks.

Kriss and the chimps escape from the van and begin walking. Before long, one of the chimps is killed when the bank it is standing on gives way. Kriss and the other chimp break into a cabin to get a little food. They are joined by an old man and meet another chimp from an abandoned pet shop. The old man is ill and Kriss lights a fire to help keep him warm. This attracts a helicopter that rescues Kriss and the old man. The chimps are left behind.

Discussion Starters and Multidisciplinary Activities

1. An earthquake is mentioned on the second page of the book and one is predicted over the radio in the second chapter. Ask students how soon they began to expect an earthquake would play a major role in the story.

2. The author chose to have one chimp killed and rescue another chimp from a pet store. Since the author started and ended the book with two chimps, why did the author choose to have one of the original chimps die? Have students discuss this.

3. Encourage students to discuss why the two chimps were left in the woods instead of rescued at the end of the story.

4. Since the time this book was published in 1981, many studies have been done teaching animals to communicate. Ask a small group of students, working with an adult volunteer or a media specialist, to find some magazine articles about these language experiments and bring them to class.

5. There have been many famous earthquakes in the United States. California has been the site of many, but there have been others. A particularly famous quake hit Yellowstone National Park. Invite a group of students to research this topic and report to the class. What was the strength of the quake? When did it occur? How much damage was done?

6. Earthquakes are measured by the Richter scale. Invite two students to learn more about this scale and have them report back to the class what they learn. What did the famous San Francisco earthquake measure on the Richter scale?

📖 *A Camel Called April*

FICTION

by Diana Hendry
Illustrated by Thor Wickstrom
New York: Lothrop, Lee & Shepard, 1990. 48p.

F H385c

This easy-to-read book will be enjoyed by primary-grade students. The text is simple and there are full-page, black-and-white drawings in each chapter. The story is told in the third person by six-year-old Harry.

Harry lives close to Vagary Park. He has always had unusual dreams, but after his bout with chicken pox, Harry's dreams are truly amazing. One night he dreams of a lion, and the next morning, when Harry looks out of his window toward the park, he sees the lion. Frightened people hang from the jungle gym until the zookeepers come and take the lion away.

That night Harry dreams of a hippopotamus, and the next day the hippo is in the fountain in the park. The zookeepers come again and they insist that this hippo is not one of theirs. Next Harry dreams of monkeys, and the monkeys are all over the park the next morning.

Harry goes to the gardener and explains to him that these animals are coming from his dreams. When Harry dreams of a giraffe, the gardener asks Harry to dream of Africa and send the giraffe back in his dream. This works. But then Harry dreams of a camel, called April, and try as he might, he cannot get the stubborn camel to go home.

The gardener and Harry come up with a plan to keep the camel as a permanent resident of the park.

Discussion Starters and Multidisciplinary Activities

1 Harry has vivid and unusual dreams. Ask for volunteers among the students to share some of the funny or unusual dreams that they have had.

2 Harry is very successful in sending the giraffe back home in his dream the next night. Did you think that Harry would be able to get rid of April easily? Why or why not?

3 Ask students if they think the plan the gardener came up with to keep April in the park is a good one, or could they think of a better plan? Share alternative plans.

4 At night, April wasn't in the park, she was in Harry's dreams. If you live near a park, ask an adult to go on a night walk with you. Cover a flashlight with red plastic. That will allow you to see, but most night animals cannot see red. After your walk, report back to the class what you saw and what sounds you heard.

5 Some students like making simple crossword puzzles. Invite a pair of students to make up a crossword puzzle for their classmates to solve. Be sure to include the word camel as one of the words in the puzzle. Students may draw the puzzle and write clues on the chalkboard.

6 Is there a park in your town or city? Does it have a special bench or statue commemorating a person or event? Ask a pair of students to research your park and report what they learn. When was it established? Who donated the land for the park? Who is responsible for keeping the park in good condition?

FICTION

Crocodile! Crocodile!
Stories Told Around the World

by Barbara Baumgartner
Illustrated by Judith Moffatt
New York: Dorling Kindersley, 1994. 45p.

This is a large-format book with bright, colored illustrations scattered throughout. It contains six folktales or legends and a chapter on staging the stories with stick puppets. It will be enjoyed by primary-grade students.

The book opens with a folktale from India, "Crocodile! Crocodile!" Offering a ride to a monkey to an island with fruit trees, the crocodile entices the monkey down to ride on his back. After the crocodile confesses that he plans to drown the monkey and eat it, the monkey tricks the crocodile to return to the monkey's home to get his heart, which he says he has left behind. In a second folktale from India, "Crocodile Hunts for the Monkey," the monkey manages to trick the crocodile again.

The third folktale, "The Squeaky Old Bed," is from Puerto Rico and involves a mouse, cat, dog, pig, and a little boy. The fourth story, "How the Chipmunk Got His Stripes," is a Native American legend. In this story, a bear boasts to a chipmunk that he can keep the sun from rising. When the bear fails in his boast, he chases the chipmunk, who leaps into a hole just as the bear claws his back, leaving dark stripes.

A folktale from China, "The Grateful Snake," and an Appalachian folktale, "Sody Saleratus," complete the stories. The final chapter makes suggestions on acting out the stories, making puppets, and presenting puppet plays.

Discussion Starters and Multidisciplinary Activities

1   The Appalachian folktale, "Sody Saleratus," may remind students of other stories, such as "Little Red Riding Hood," and "The Three Billy Goats Gruff." Ask students to tell in which way "Sody Saleratus" resembles other stories that they know.

2   The first two stories have the same characters, a clever monkey and a determined crocodile. Ask students to discuss another plan the crocodile might come up with to catch the monkey. Do they think the crocodile will ever succeed?

3   After reading "The Grateful Snake," ask students to discuss what they think made Zee suspicious of his brother, Chu.

4   Using ideas from "Bringing the Stories to Life with Stick Puppets," invite small groups of students to prepare and present folktales and legends included in this book.

5   If your school has cooking facilities, students might want to make baking powder biscuits after reading "Sody Saleratus." One student might supply a recipe, and other students can volunteer to bring the various ingredients needed. Teams can help with the preparation, baking, serving, and cleanup.

6   Many students are fascinated with dragons. There is a picture of one on page 26. Invite interested students to draw their own dragon pictures, using whichever medium they prefer. Share the dragon pictures. If any of the students wish to write a story to go along with their dragon picture, encourage them to do so.

📖 *The Elephant in the Dark*

FICTION

by Carol Carrick
Illustrated by Donald Carrick
New York: Clarion Books, 1988. 135p.

F C 234e

This chapter book is illustrated by a few black-and-white drawings. It is set in the early 1800s in Massachusetts and is told from the point of view of twelve-year-old Will. The story will be enjoyed by readers in third through fifth grades.

Will lives alone with his mother in poverty. He enjoys his time at home but hates school, where he always seems to be the butt of student jokes. He can read well and do his sums, so school is not hard for him, it is just unpleasant.

Will's mother, Maddy, is very ill. She is an unconventional woman who does not care what other people think. She has a strong love of nature and, when she is not ill, is able to weave baskets and do beautiful paintings.

One night when Maddy is so sick that she is spitting up blood, Will goes for help to the storeowners, Mr. and Mrs. Sanderson. They had hired Will to work for them before school in the mornings. They bring a doctor and try to help, but Will's mother dies.

Will stops going to school and goes to live and work at the Sanderson's. One day a stranger arrives with an elephant. The stranger leaves, promising to return in the spring and pay for the elephant's keep. Will grows fond of the elephant, Toong, who learns to like and obey him. In the spring when an acrobat comes to claim Toong, Will leaves the Sanderson's, follows the acrobat, and eventually is allowed to travel with them.

Discussion Starters and Multidisciplinary Activities

1 Will both loved his mother and sometimes felt ashamed of her. Ask students to discuss situations where they sometimes have conflicting feelings.

2 The Sanderson's take Will in and treat him well. Ask students what they think would have happened if Will had let Toong go and chose to remain with the Sanderson's.

3 At the end of the story, Will has joined up with Franzini and is off to Boston. Invite students to discuss what they think will eventually happen to Will.

4 At one point when he thinks he has lost Toong, Will says that he will grow up and earn enough money to buy her. Knowing that will take time, he wonders how long elephants live. Ask a pair of students to research and report what they learn. How long does a typical elephant in captivity live? How much would it cost to buy an elephant?

5 On page 135, the author tells about the true events surrounding an elephant called Old Bet. Have a small group of students research the beginnings of the traveling circus in the United States and report what they learn to the class.

6 There is a poster about Franzini on page 102. Have students design a poster featuring Toong and Will. The poster should be in the form of the announcement of a performance and it should include a picture as well as the lettering. Put the completed posters on the wall so that classmates may enjoy them.

From *Exploring the World of Animals*. © 1997. Teacher Ideas Press. (800) 237-6124.

The Great American Elephant Chase

FICTION

by Gillian Cross
New York: Holiday House, 1992. 193p.

F C8838g

This chapter book, without illustrations, chronicles the journey of two young people and an elephant from Pennsylvania to Nebraska. It will be enjoyed by fourth- and fifth-grade readers.

Tad, an orphan, lives with his aunt in a boarding house. He is a quiet and insecure boy. As the story opens, Esther, the hired girl, manages to push Tad down the stairs, making a big mess and pretending it is all Tad's fault. Tad goes out for cleaning supplies and stops at the train station to see a performing elephant that has come to town.

Tad hides to avoid Esther and ends up leaving on the train in the elephant car. He meets the elephant's owner, Michael Keenan, one of Mr. Keenan's daughters, Cissie, and the elephant, Khush.

Since Tad's life has been miserable, he decides to travel with Mr. Keenan for a while, tending the elephant.

At one point, Tad and Khush go ahead on an earlier train. Tad learns that Mr. Keenan and many others have been killed in a wreck involving the train behind them. Cissie survives, and Mr. Jackson, a boarder from Markle accompanied by Esther, appear, holding a piece of paper indicating Khush belongs to them.

Cissie is determined to take Khush with her to Ketty's house in Nebraska, where she now hopes to live. Tad helps Cissie on her journey with the elephant down the Monongahela and Ohio Rivers, up the Missssippi and Missouri, and by foot across Nebraska, being pursued all the way by Esther and Mr. Jackson.

Discussion Starters and Multidisciplinary Activities

1 Ask readers if they believed that Cissie underwent a miraculous cure when she drank the green medicine or were suspicious that this was a trick orchestrated by Michael Keenan?

2 Over and over, Ketty's house and gardens in Nebraska are described. In reality, Ketty's house and land was quite different from the description. Have readers discuss the differences between the two.

3 When the story ends, a new way of life is starting for Tad and Khush. Ask students to discuss what they think Tad will do first.

4 Khush is described as an Indian elephant. Ask two students to research elephants. What is the difference between Indian and African elephants? On a map, have these students point out to the class where both types of elephants live and explain how they are similar and different.

5 Invite interested students to write an original chapter 31 to add to this book. It could begin just where the book ends and describe what Tad and Khush do next, or it could take the form of a letter from Tad to Cissie describing what has happened to Tad and Khush since leaving Ketty's house.

6 One problem faced by Tad and Cissie was finding enough water to drink while they crossed Nebraska. Invite two students to research the needs of elephants. How much water do they drink a day? How much food do they eat a day?

 *Jaguarundi*

FICTION

by Virginia Hamilton
Paintings by Floyd Cooper
New York: Scholastic, Blue Sky Press, 1995. 36p.

This book contains outstanding, full-color paintings and will appeal to readers of all ages. In addition to the story, which is a fantasy following Rundi Jaguarundi as he flees his rain forest home to seek a new home, the reader is introduced to a variety of real rain forest animals.

Rundi Jaguarundi realizes that the rain forest canopy is disappearing as settlers clear timber and build homes, barns, and fences. He invites Coati Coatimundi to join him in leaving and seeking a new home. Coati accepts the invitation. They also decide to meet at the Great Pineapple Field and say good-bye to friends and invite others to join them in moving north.

Kit Fox, Owl Monkey, Bush Dog, Spotted Cavy, Maned Wolf, Howler Monkey, White-throated Capuchin Monkey, Ringtail Cat, White-tailed Deer, Big Brown Bat, Ocelot, and Bobcat all come to say good-bye to their friends. Although most of these animals are worried, none want to leave. They will hide, try to adapt, and admit that perhaps in time they will be forced to leave.

When Rundi and Coati reach the Rio Bravo, they are dismayed to see settlers, cats, and dogs. They cross the river and Rundi finds a red jaguarundi and makes a den in a thicket. For the time being, he is content to stay put. Coati is also content. He stays by himself but is happy to see a band of coatamundis.

Discussion Starters and Multidisciplinary Activities

1   The first animal that Rundi asks to leave with him to seek a new home in the north is Coati. Coati agrees. Why do you think this one animal is ready to move away when none of the others are?

2   Before saying good-bye to friends, the animals choose to meet and discuss their problem in the Great Pineapple Field of the Fallen Timber. Why is this an appropriate meeting place?

3   Big Brown Bat suggests that they should stay put and adapt to changes. Ask students if they think Big Brown Bat is right or wrong? Is staying put a good choice for Brown Bat but not a good choice for Jaguarundi?

4   This story could make an excellent script for a puppet show. Invite students to make puppets representing the main characters and have them talk about their rain forest home and the reasons why they must move north.

5   When all of the animals meet to say farewell, it is a strange and mysterious setting. Ask a few interested students to decide what might make good background music for this scene if it were to be turned into a video. Have them record three minutes of music, or bird calls and sounds, and play this for the class.

6   Rundi and Coati finally cross the Rio Bravo or Rio Grande. Ask a pair of students to research and show the route on a map that these two animals might have taken while seeking a new home.

📖 *Kalinzu, A Story from Africa*

FICTION

by Jeremy Grimsdell
New York: Kingfisher Books, 1993. 28p. *FG884K*

This story is illustrated with full-color pastel drawings and will appeal to primary-grade students. There are about thirty words of text per page.

Kalinzu is a small water buffalo who lives on the grasslands of East Africa with her mother, Amani. Kalinzu is only one month old, so she seldom goes far from her mother's side. When the day is hot, Kalinzu likes to watch the large bull buffalo sink into cool, muddy pools. But she does not like the red-billed oxpeckers, birds who perch on her back and look for ticks to eat.

One night, Kalinzu and Amani drop a short distance behind the herd when Kalinzu stops to watch an aardvark at a termite mound. Three hyenas take this opportunity to form a circle and attack. Amani protects Kalinzu, who screams out in terror. This scream brings the rest of the herd thundering toward them. The hyenas flee.

But Kalinzu, in panic, rushes into a thicket and knocks herself out. When Amani searches for her baby, she is unable to find her and Kalinzu, unconscious, makes no noise. The herd moves on.

When Kalinzu wakes up she is frightened and does not know where her mother and the herd have gone. Two red-billed oxpeckers land on her back. When they fly away, Kalinzu follows them and they lead her back to her mother who greets her with joy.

Discussion Starters and Multidisciplinary Activities

1   In the beginning of the story, Kalinzu tries everything to shake the oxpeckers off of her back. As the story ends, there is an oxpecker riding on Kalinzu's back and she is not trying to get rid of it. Have students explain Kalinzu's change of attitude toward the red-billed oxpeckers.

2   Ask students what they thought might happen when the three hyenas appeared, surrounding Kalinzu and her mother.

3   Ask students to discuss what they think might have happened to Kalinzu if she had not been able to find her mother and rejoin the herd the next day.

4   On a map of the world, have students find East Africa and point out what countries are located there.

5   Many other animals besides water buffalo are pictured in this book. With the help of the media specialist or an adult volunteer, have a small group of students do some research on these animals and report back to the class what they learn. The students might be given a chart to complete: name of animal, size, what it eats, where it lives, how big it is, its enemies. Creatures for research might include: a giraffe, a warthog, a rhinoceros, hyenas, and aardvarks.

6   A pair of interested students might want to solve a mystery. Several animals appear in the book that are not identified by name. Invite two students, with the help of an adult volunteer, to identify at least two of the animals pictured in this book that are not identified in the text.

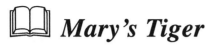 *Mary's Tiger*

FICTION

by Rex Harley
Illustrated by Sue Porter
San Diego: Harcourt Brace, 1990. 28p.

This picture book has a very simple text and colorful, humorous illustrations. It will be enjoyed by students in kindergarten through second grade. Part of the book is realistic and part fantasy. It will lend itself to group discussion.

Mary is a little girl who loves painting. One day her teacher, Mrs. Morris, suggests that Mary fill her whole page with a colorful picture. Mary is delighted to paint her favorite animal, a tiger. She begins by painting a huge head and finds that because the head is so big, there is very little room left on the paper for the tiger's body.

Mary paints a body with stripes and tiny legs and tail. Mary thinks that her tiger looks a little unhappy because it is so scrunched up. She paints a big smile on the tiger's face.

When she goes home to her family, each one notices the tiger and asks about the smile. Mother wonders if the tiger is smiling because it is in love. Mary's father asks if the tiger has just had a tasty meal. Mary's brother, Paul, asks if the tiger is laughing at Mary. But Mary answers "no" to all these questions.

Mary's mother wants to hang the tiger picture in the kitchen, but Mary takes it to her bedroom and hangs it on the wall there. Grin, the tiger, is not comfortable when the room gets dark. He wiggles and twists around. Grin finally pushes off the picture and sleeps on Mary's pillow.

Discussion Starters and Multidisciplinary Activities

1 Ask students at what point this story stopped being a realistic story and turned into a fantasy?

2 Invite students to explain their ideas about why Mary took the sheet of drawing paper, after Grin had left it, crumpled it up, and threw it away.

3 Since the drawing paper is gone, have students discuss whether Grin has gone. If they think that he has not gone away, where is he now?

4 Invite the class to make their own colorful pictures of a favorite animal. They may paint like Mary did, or they may use colored pencils, magic markers, or crayons. When they are complete, you might want to put them in a favorite animal book.

5 Some wild animals, such as tigers, perform in circuses. Each student in the class might enjoy adding a car to a circus train. On background paper, paint a train engine and track. Ask each student to bring a shoebox. Tack the bottom of each shoebox to the bulletin board on the track. Students should bring in cloth or plastic zoo animals, or paper cutouts, that are 4 inches or less tall. Have each student set an animal in a shoebox and cut slits, like spaces between bars, in the lid of the shoebox. Put the lids back on the boxes to represent cages.

6 With the help of a media specialist or adult volunteer, have a small group of students research where tigers live and then share what they learn.

From *Exploring the World of Animals.* © 1997. Teacher Ideas Press. (800) 237-6124.

📖 *Nanta's Search for Lion*

FICTION

by Suse MacDonald
New York: Morrow Junior Books, 1995. Unpaged.

This picture book, presented in a die-cut format, is a story and game in one. The text is simple and the illustrations colorful. It will be enjoyed by kindergarten through second-grade students.

Nanta is a child who lives in a Maasai village in Africa. She has heard hunters tell stories about a lion that roams the plains and steals cattle from them. Nanta wants to see the lion herself. She slips quietly out of the village, taking a gourd filled with milk, and begins walking.

When Nanta arrives at a grove of thorn trees, she sees two birds looking for ticks on a giraffe's back, but she sees no lion. She climbs up high on a termite mound and sees a water buffalo and two gazelles. She also sees an old hippopotamus soaking in the water hole. But there is no lion.

In a neighboring village, Nanta sees a stork and a goat. Nanta visits with her friends and then heads back home disappointed that she has not seen the lion. She does see some monkeys playing in the trees, and she startles two parrots who flap their wings and fly away.

By this point in the story, Nanta is thirsty, so she sits down to drink her milk. The text says, "She never did see the lion. Did you?" And on this page the reader sees a beautiful lion that has been only partially observable for several pages but can now be seen in its entirety.

Discussion Starters and Multidisciplinary Activities

1 Students will enjoy seeing how parts of one picture are revealed or concealed on the next page by the use of die-cuts. Ask students when they first saw part of Nanta's lion.

2 Have students discuss why no one in the neighboring village seemed surprised or alarmed when Nanta arrived alone.

3 Nanta took a gourd filled with milk when she set off on her long walk. Ask students what they take with them when they go on a long hike and how they carry it.

4 In the first picture of Nanta, she is wearing an elaborate necklace. Ask a small group of students, working with a media specialist or adult volunteer, to find out more about the Maasai. If possible they should bring a photograph from a book or magazine which shows some of the tribe's jewelry.

5 Ask a pair of students to work with the media specialist to find out where the Maasai live in Africa, and have the students display the location of the tribe on a map.

6 The author of this book, Suse MacDonald, has written and illustrated other books. One of these, *Alphabatics,* was named a Caldecott Honor Book. Ask a pair of students, with the help of the school media specialist, to locate *Alphabatics* and to learn about the Caldecott Award. The students should explain to their classmates what the award represents and share some of the pictures from *Alphabatics.*

FICTION

📖 *Sungura and Leopard, A Swahili Trickster Tale*

by Barbara Knutson
Boston: Little, Brown, 1993. 28p.

This book is a retelling of a story from Tanzania and Malawi. The bright illustrations are a combination of watercolor and ink on scratchboard. It will be enjoyed by second- and third-grade readers.

Sungura and Leopard decide almost at the same moment that the time has come for each of them to build a home, and they pick the exact same spot. Leopard goes to gather sticks for the foundation and puts a bundle on the hill. Sungura gathers sticks and puts them next to the first bundle thinking that his ancestors are helping with the house building. When Leopard sees more sticks than he can account for, he blames it on his poor counting and thinks that his ancestors are helping him, too.

Throughout the whole building process Sungura and Leopard never see one another. They continue to build, each believing that ancestors are helping them. The very night the house is finished, both animals crawl inside and fall asleep.

In the morning, both animals are surprised. Because both animals had worked hard and neither was willing to leave, they divide the house in half with a thin wall between them. But Sungura and his wife and children wish there were a way to get rid of their dangerous neighbor. They pretend Sungura is a great hunter who can kill elephants and leopards. The trick works and Leopard leaves the home to the hares.

Discussion Starters and Multidisciplinary Activities

1 Ask students if, in the beginning of the story, they thought that Leopard and Sungura could really live happily together in the same house, or did they think one would have to leave?

2 Have students discuss how Sungura was able to twist around the fact that Baboon advised Leopard to return to his house in such a way that he could use that against Leopard, too.

3 Ask students if they have read other "trickster" tales where one creature, usually a small and helpless one, outwits a larger, stronger one. Have students discuss these tales.

4 The end papers in this book look like a series of prints. Students might want to try printmaking using potatoes. A student will need half of a potato. * On the cut surface, the student draws a simple animal shape and then cuts away the potato so that the animal shape is left standing out from the rest of the potato. The potato can now be dipped in paint and can be used to stamp the design on paper.

5 Have two students locate Tanzania and Malawi (countries where this story originated) and point them out on the map to classmates.

6 Rabbit families do not live in houses like the one pictured in this book. Invite a small group of students to find out how and where rabbit families normally live.

---

*Review with children all safety precautions about using knives before letting them do this!

From *Exploring the World of Animals*. © 1997. Teacher Ideas Press. (800) 237-6124.

📖 ***The Talking Earth***

by Jean Craighead George
New York: Harper & Row, 1983. 151p.

F G292th

FICTION

This contemporary story, set in Florida, is told from the viewpoint of a young Seminole Indian girl, Billie Wind. It will be enjoyed by fourth- and fifth-grade readers.

When the story begins, Billie Wind is being scolded for her failure to believe in ancient Indian stories about talking animals and little people who live under the earth. Although Billie Wind lives with her tribe in the Florida Everglades and observes their customs, she has been to the Kennedy Space Center School and holds a more modern view of the world.

When the council asks what punishment she should have, Billie Wind suggests that she go into the pa-hay-okee, the Everglades where the spirits dwell, and hear the animals talk. The council agrees, and Billie Wind is soon alone in the Everglades.

A fire sweeps across the area and Billie Wind takes refuge in a cave she finds in a sinkhole. She stays there for several days until the ground is cool enough for her to walk on. She makes friends with Petang, a little otter. They find enough fish to keep them alive. When they go to leave, Billie Wind finds that her boat has burned. She and Petang make do with food they find in the wild while Billie Wind fashions a new boat.

Before she gets safely back to her people, Billie Wind tames a panther, learns from a turtle, and makes friends with an American Indian boy who is on his own quest.

Discussion Starters and Multidisciplinary Activities

1   For most of this story Billie Wind is alone with various animals in the swamp. Only during the last few pages does another human enter the story. Ask students why they think the author introduced the character of Oats?

2   The three animals that Billie Wind grew close to on her adventures were Petang, Cootchobee, and Burden. These animals were different from one another. Ask students to discuss what Billie Wind learned from each of the animals.

3   Part of Billie Wind's success in the swamps was due to her mother putting some very useful items in Billie Wind's dugout. Ask the students to discuss what was in the dugout and how these things were vital to Billie Wind.

4   The story describes "panther" as the animal that Billie Wind befriends. Ask a pair of students to research this subject. What panthers still live in Florida? How many are left? Is there another, more common name for the Florida panther?

5   A hurricane hits at the end of the story. Billie Wind says this is the first hurricane she has lived through. Ask some interested students to research this. On average, how many hurricanes hit Florida each year? Which ones are famous for the destruction caused. Students should report to the class what they learn.

6   Burden was a gopher turtle. Ask a small group of students to research the gopher turtle and report what they learn. Where do these turtles live? How big do they grow?

Animals in the Wild

◆ *Bridges and Poetry* ◆

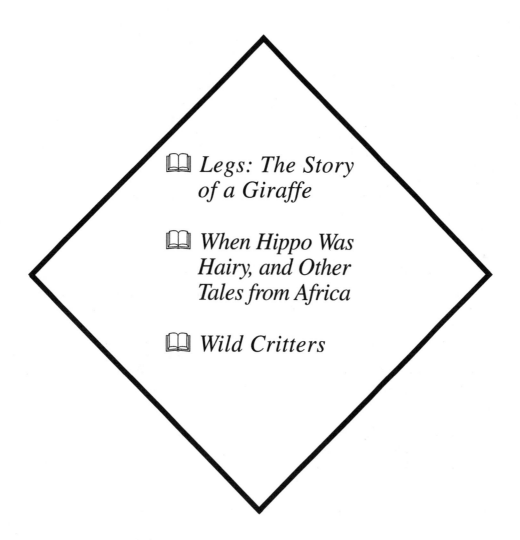

 Legs: The Story of a Giraffe

 When Hippo Was Hairy, and Other Tales from Africa

Wild Critters

Legs: The Story of a Giraffe

**BRIDGES
AND POETRY**

by Phyllis Barber
Illustrated by Ann Baumann
New York: Margaret K. McElderry Books, 1991. 71p.

This chapter book is illustrated with lovely black-and-white sketches and will be enjoyed by third- through fifth-grade readers. As a bridge book, it has both a story line and includes much factual information.

This story begins with the birth of a giraffe, Imburugutu, in Kenya. His mother and other auntie cows take care of him. Imburugutu plays with the other calves, chews leaves, and is saved from a lion attack by an auntie cow.

The main enemy of the giraffes are hunters, *wawindaji*. One day Imburugutu hears a gunshot and sees his mother fall. After that, Imburugutu misses his mother but continues to grow and thrive. Then one day hunters catch him in their net.

He is taken for a long truck ride to the sea, where he is loaded on a freighter. Imburugutu is kept in a cage with an open top because he is so tall. On the freighter he is kept on deck because of his height. He lives through a fierce storm and is finally taken to holding pens outside a zoo.

He is checked, found healthy, moved to the giraffe house, and given the name Sun Dancer. Among the other three giraffes is Spotted Jacket, who is particularly unfriendly. One rainy day, Spotted Jacket fights with Sun Dancer who slips in the mud. His feet slide so far apart that he cannot stand. By the time help comes, it is too late, and Sun Dancer dies.

Possible Topics for Further Investigation

1 In an afterword to the book, it is noted that zoo animals are rarely imported from the wild now. Most zoos trade with other zoos and breed their animals in captivity. Have a small group of students find the name and address of the zoo closest to you. These students should write the curator of the zoo and ask for information about their giraffes. How many do they have? What are their names? Were the giraffes born in the zoo or were they traded to the zoo from another place? The students should enclose a stamped, self-addressed envelope and should share whatever information they receive.

2 Sun Dancer looks different from the other giraffes in the zoo. Invite a small group of interested students to find out how many kinds of giraffes there are and what each type looks like. The students should clip, photocopy, or draw pictures of each type and share their information with the class.

3 Imburugutu speaks Swahili. A small group of students might want to research and find out more about the countries and languages of Africa. Have the students make a chart in which they list all of the countries alphabetically that are located in modern Africa and the language(s) that are spoken in these countries. The students should post their chart and share information with the class, showing the African countries on a map.

When Hippo Was Hairy, and Other Tales from Africa

by Nick Greaves
Illustrated by Rod Clement
New York: Barrons, 1988. 144p.

This book contains maps as well as realistic black-and-white and color drawings. It includes several sections about different wild animals. In each section there are one or more tales followed by facts about the animals. This makes it a perfect "bridge" book, combining the elements of storytelling with nonfiction. It will be enjoyed by readers in grades three through five.

The author, Nick Greaves, lives in Zimbabwe and has written traditional animal stories from many different African tribes. Among the animals included are lions, hares, leopards, cheetahs, wild dogs, hyenas, jackals, elephants, rhinos, buffaloes, baboons, giraffes, crocodiles, waterbucks, zebras, tsessebes, wart hogs, dassies, ostriches, and tortoises.

The stories come from the following tribes or sources: Batonka, Hmbakushu, Ndebele, Bushman, Zulu, Shona, Swaziland, Hottentot, East Africans, a Makushu story from the Okavango, the Angoni of Central Africa, Swazi, Xhosa, Sesotho, and Masai.

In the "Facts About . . ." section following each folktale there is a map showing the location where the animal lives and information about the animal, including its height and weight when full grown, weight at birth, number of young, gestation period, age at weaning and at maturity, and life span.

Possible Topics for Further Investigation

1 Ask students to discuss which animals in this book were new to them. (Many will point out the waterbuck, tsessebe, wart hogs, and dassie.) Invite small groups of students who are interested in the same animal to research more about the animal and perhaps find pictures of it. Encourage these small groups to share what they learn.

2 Oral storytelling is a great skill. Invite interested students to pick out a favorite tale from this book and practice telling it in their own words. When prepared, let the student storytellers tell their stories to this or another class. Some participating students might want to present their material as flannelboard stories. To do this, they will need to make the pictures that they want to put on the flannelboard as they tell their tales. These pictures can be drawn and colored on pellon, which is easy to find in fabric stores and is good for this purpose because it sticks nicely to felt.

3 In the "Facts About . . ." section, habitats for each animal are described. Interested students might design and create a habitat for one of the animals using cutouts or small plastic animals, dirt, and grass, and by arranging the material in an open shoebox set on its side. These dioramas should be labeled and a collection of them might be placed on display.

 *Wild Critters*

verse by Tim Jones
Photography by Tom Walker
Portland, OR: Graphics Art Center, 1992. 48p.

This book is illustrated with striking, color photographs. Unlike many collections of poetry, all of the poems are written by one poet. It will be enjoyed by elementary school students.

The poems include: The sound of silence, A yawn dawning, Caribou Carrie, One stuck duck, Back seat loonacy, The view forever, Camouflage, Oh, for a hide to hide in, Sea otter transit authority, The Arctic waterbed, Flower child, Poor George bear, Peekaboo caribou, Determined ermine, Pfine pfeathered pfashion, The terrible twos, Snorkeling, Cooling your wheels, Cool courage, and Whatever can a walrus do?

Some elementary school students appreciate poetry, while others profess not to like it. Students often think poetry must use stilted language and traditional subject matter. Students who usually do not like poetry may respond to the light touch used in this book.

The poems in this book are different lengths, ranging from four to twenty-eight lines. All include the use of rhyme and most have a humorous aspect, including unusual titles. Although the poems are written about birds and animals, at least a few of the poems could equally describe people if the animal photograph were simply omitted.

Discussion Starters and Multidisciplinary Activities

1   Read "Back seat loonacy" to the students. What do they think is happening in the poem? (Most will think that it describes a child in the backseat of a car who is eager for the drive to be over.) Then show them the picture. Are the students surprised?

2   Explain to students that two words can be spelled the same but have different meanings. Ask them to find a multiple-meaning word in the poem on page 22 about the white moose.

3   Invite interested students to add two stanzas to "The sound of silence" in the manner of the original verses (which discuss geese in spring and fall). The two new verses should talk about geese in summer and winter.

4   Students may be quite surprised to look at the pictures on pages 21 and 37, which compare the appearance of a willow ptarmigan in winter, summer, and spring. Ask a pair of students to research this bird. Where do ptarmigan live? What do they eat? What are their enemies? How does their color change prove useful to them?

5   This book contains a photo of a white moose. Have a pair of students research albinos in the animal world and report what they learn.

6   The weasel pictured on page 35 is also known as an ermine. Have a pair of students report to their classmates on the color changes in ermine and how the fur of this animal has been used.

Animals in the Wild

Nonfiction Connections

 Africa's Animal Giants

 Arctic Tundra

The Caribou

Endangered Animal Babies

The Endangered Florida Panther

Endangered Savannah Animals

Kangaroos on Location

Lion

Primates: Lemurs, Monkeys, and You

Tiger, Tiger, Growing Up

To the Top of the World, Adventures with Arctic Wolves

📖 *Africa's Animal Giants*

by Jane R. McCauley

Washington, DC: The National Geographic Society, 1987. 34p.

This book is part of the Books For Young Explorers series prepared by the National Geographic Society. It has a simple text and is illustrated with color photographs. The book will be enjoyed by second- and third-grade readers.

On the continent of Africa, one can find some of the biggest wild animals on Earth. First, there are herds of elephants who stop to drink and bathe at a water hole. These elephants, largest of the land animals, have followed one another across the open plain and often must go for several days without water. The text and pictures show the ways in which an elephant uses its trunk.

Next the reader learns about lions, the largest cats in Africa. The lions live in prides and hunt herds of animals such as zebras. They are also shown peacefully sleeping in trees.

Ostriches, the largest of all birds, are shown next. They cannot fly but can run fast on long legs. Then the reader meets the rhinoceros, a huge animal with horns on its nose, and the hippopotamus, shown walking underwater on a rocky river bottom. A herd of muddy hippos, looking like giant, muddy rocks, are pictured together in the river. The mud helps to keep their skin from drying out. A Cape buffalo is also shown rolling in the mud. The book concludes with a section on giraffes, the tallest of all animals, and gorillas, that live in shady forests, high in the mountains.

Possible Topics for Further Investigation

1   Many of the animals shown in this book are endangered. Ask a pair of students to learn more about endangered species. What does it mean to be endangered? Who prepares this list of endangered species? How is an animal placed on it? How often is the list updated? What effect does it have on people and animals (hunting laws, etc.) when an animal is placed on the endangered species list? Can the students get and share a current list of endangered species?

2   The rhinoceros and the elephant are so big that it would seem they have no enemies. In fact, humans are their enemies. Both rhinos and elephants are hunted for their horns and tusks. Ask a pair of students to research this topic. Who hunts these animals? What are the rhino's horns used for? The elephant's tusks? Are there any laws protecting these animals and regulating the sales of items made from horns and tusks? Give the students time to report orally to the class.

3   Writing a story from an unusual point of view could be fun for students. Ask them to choose an animal near a watering hole in Africa and describe what goes on from that animal's point of view. They might write from the point of view of a thirsty elephant who has just walked across the plains, from the point of view of a lion planning to attack a nearby herd of zebra, or from the point of view of an egret perched atop the head of a Cape buffalo. Share the stories with the class.

Arctic Tundra

by Donald M. Silver
Illustrated by Patricia J. Wynne
New York: W. H. Freeman, 1994. 48p.

NONFICTION CONNECTIONS

This book is one of a series of Scientific American Books for Young Readers under the grouping of "one small square." The purpose of the books is to give the reader a close look at one small square of the earth. Filled with color illustrations and diagrams, this book will be enjoyed by readers in grades two through five. There is an index and titles for suggested additional reading.

The book begins with riddles about the tundra. The tundra explored in this book is in the Arctic, one of the coldest parts of the earth. The first half shows the tundra in winter, and then in summer.

A wide variety of birds and animals are featured, including polar bears, caribou, lichen moths, gyrfalcon, ravens, ptarmigan, snowshoe hares, arctic redpolls, musk oxen, snowy owls, foxes, wolves, lemmings, ground squirrels, loons, swans, and grizzly bears.

Several scientific experiments for students are suggested in marginal notes in the book. These require only a minimum of equipment to carry out at home or in the classroom.

There is a chapter on tundra plants that seem to hug the ground. A full grown tree may be only four inches tall. Many of the tundra plants grow together in thick mats. They have a very short growing season.

Possible Topics for Further Investigation

1. Using pages 40 through 43 in this book, a group of students could prepare an attractive and informative bulletin board. It could picture a map in the center with arrows showing where the arctic tundra is located. Students could select and devote portions of the board to tundra life including: mammals, fishes and amphibians, invertebrates, monera, funguses, protists, and plants. Students could draw and label pictures of their favorites.

2. Some birds and animals undergo a striking color change during the seasons of the year. One that is featured in this book is the ptarmigan. Ask a pair of students to provide color illustrations of the ptarmigan in various seasons. These students should try to find one or two other examples of birds or animals that "put on a winter coat" and share these.

3. You can carry out the experiment suggested in the book on page 16 if you live in a snowy area. Take two thermometers. On a snowy day, put one thermometer outside and place it on the ground where it will not be disturbed. Tie the other thermometer to a long stick and push it deep into a snow bank (with the end of the stick above the snow so you can find it again). Wait several hours. Then come back and read the temperature on both thermometers. If you were an arctic lemming where would you want to be on a snowy day, on top of the ground or underneath the ground? Why?

The Caribou

by Lorle K. Harris
Minneapolis: Dillon, 1988. 60p.

NONFICTION CONNECTIONS

This book is part of Dillon's Remarkable Animals series. It is illustrated with color photographs and will appeal to third- through fifth-grade readers. The book contains four chapters, a glossary, and an index.

In the introduction, "Facts About the Caribou," the reader learns that caribou range throughout the arctic and the subarctic regions of North America, Scandinavia, and Asia.

Barren-ground caribou and reindeer migrate hundreds of miles each year. They live on sedges, grasses, mushrooms, and lichens. The treeless plain that is home to caribou and reindeer is called tundra.

Caribou are members of the deer family and, like deer, are ruminants. Instead of upper front teeth, they have a hard pad that they use to break up food before swallowing. Their stomach is four-chambered and caribou are cud chewers. They grow antlers that are shed each year. Their hoofs are built to plow through snow.

Barren-ground caribou move in herds of thousands as they travel between winter and summer ranges. The woodland caribou, which now number only two thousand, live in northern Idaho and in four of the Canadian provinces. Peary's caribous are much smaller than the others and live in wooded areas on arctic islands in the far north. Reindeer are found in Scandinavia and parts of the former Soviet Union.

Possible Topics for Further Investigation

1 Humans have proved to be serious enemies of the caribou. Have a pair of students write to the Alaska and Idaho Departments of Fish and Game to request pamphlets and information about caribou. The students should be certain to include a large, self-addressed, stamped envelope that can be used for reply. If the students do receive pamphlets, allow time for them to share.

2 Many geographic areas are named in this book. Ask a small group of interested students to locate the following areas and label them on a world map: British Columbia, Ontario, Manitoba, Newfoundland, Idaho, Maine, the Arctic Circle, Mount McKinley, the Yukon Territory, Alaska, Prudhoe Bay, the Arctic Ocean, Prince William Sound, the Caniapiscau River, and the Selkirk Mountains.

3 Caribou, like cows, are ruminants, animals that have four-chamber stomachs and that chew cud. Ask a small group of students to study ruminants. These students should make a large, colored diagram of the caribou's four-chamber stomach and be able to explain how it works. What other animals are ruminants? Do their stomachs work in the same way? How does the stomach of a ruminant differ from the stomach of a carnivore such as a lion? (Students might want to make a diagram of a lion's stomach also to show the difference.) Allow time for these students to share what they learned.

📖 *Endangered Animal Babies*

by Thane Maynard
New York: Franklin Watts, 1993. 60p.

This is a Cincinnati Zoo Book presented by Franklin Watts in collaboration with the Cincinnati Zoo and Botanical Gardens. It is a large-format book with color photographs and will be enjoyed by students in third through fifth grades.

This book presents profiles of twenty-four species which zoos and animal research centers have joined together to save from extinction through an international rescue effort known as Species Survival Plan (SSP). Under this plan, captive breeding programs are used to build healthy populations of each endangered species.

Each of the twenty-four animals is presented, along with native range maps, tables of vital facts, descriptions of how these animals develop and grow, and why they need help in order to survive.

The book includes the following animals: gray bats, Texas blind salamanders, bald eagles, American alligators, ocelots, manatees, spectacled bears, hyacinth macaws, blue whales, zebra duikers, colobus monkeys, radiated tortoises, tomato frogs, bongo antelopes, giant elands, Siamang gibbons, birdwing butterflys, Guam rails, banded linsangs, reticulated pythons, fishing cats, Indian rhinoceroses, shoebill storks, lowland gorillas, peregrine falcons, American burying beetles, and barn owls.

The book contains a glossary of terms and suggested books and magazines for further reading.

Possible Topics for Further Investigation

1. Among its suggestions for further reading this book mentions *International Wildlife* magazine and *National Wildlife* magazine. See if your school or public library, a parent, or a staff member subscribes to one or both of these magazines. Borrow some back issues and put them on a "research table." Encourage individual students to browse through these magazines, choose an article of interest, and write a short report on what they have learned. These reports could then be posted on a "wildlife bulletin board."

2. A pair of students might want to write to your closest zoo and ask them if they participate in the Species Survival Plan (SSP). If they do not, ask if they can supply the name and address of the closest zoo that does participate. Ask for more information about SSP. If a zoo is near you, perhaps someone from the zoo could visit and talk about this plan. If you are located some distance from a large participating zoo, send a self-addressed, stamped envelope and request pamphlets or other available information to share with the class.

3. Encourage a small group of students to combine their talents to make a board game that class members can play. To advance on the trail of this wildlife board game, students will roll a die and move that many spaces forward *if* they can answer a question on a card from the top of a deck of cards. The students will prepare animal wildlife questions on cards (with short answers on the back) as the playing deck for this wildlife board game.

The Endangered Florida Panther

by Margaret Goff Clark
New York: Cobblehill Books, 1993. 54p.

This book is illustrated with excellent color photographs and will be enjoyed by students in grades three through five.

The book is divided into nine chapters: "How the Panther Lives," "Panther History," "Collaring a Panther," "Surprise Encounter," "Alligator Alley," "Mystery of Cat Number 12," "Is There Hope?" "Captive Breeding," and "To See a Panther." There is also an index.

At one time the Florida panther lived throughout the southeastern United States ranging from Texas to the Atlantic coast and as far north as Tennessee. Now it is endangered. A map shows its present home indicating the preserves, parks, and refuges in southern Florida.

One section tells about panthers' daily lives. Much of this information was gathered by monitoring radio-collared panthers. Attaching a collar is a major job with at least four people involved. A huntsman with dogs trees the panther. The other team members spread out a cushion filled with trash bags on the ground beneath the panther. A specialist shoots a dart with anesthetic appropriate for the size of the panther. The panther then falls or is lowered into a net strung just above the cushion. The panther is checked by a vet and a collar is attached so that the animal can be tracked.

Actions, such as laws to prevent people from shooting panthers, captive breeding, and underpasses to minimize road kill, make it possible for the panther population to increase.

Possible Topics for Further Investigation

1 Invite a pair of students to make a large map of Florida. They should include some of the major cities, lakes, and rivers. Have them indicate "Alligator Alley" on their map and the following other areas: Fakahatchee Strand State Preserve, Florida Panther Wildlife Refuge, Big Cypress National Preserve, Loxahatchee National Wildlife Refuge, and the Everglades National Park. Hang the map in the classroom so that other students can refer to it.

2 A group of students might plan a simple fund-raiser, such as a noon popcorn sale at school, to raise money to help the Florida panther. For information, or to send a donation, students should write to the Florida Panther Research and Management Trust Fund, Florida Game and Fresh Water Fish Commission, 620 South Meridian Street, Tallahassee, FL 32399-1600. A check should be made payable to the Florida Game and Fresh Water Fish Commission noting that it is for the Trust Fund.

3 Not only the Florida panther, but the western cougar has also had a hard time surviving. The cougar, or mountain lion, also had a bounty placed on its head in several western states, including California, because farmers and ranchers feared that mountain lions would destroy livestock and could pose a hazard to dogs and humans. Have a small group of students research this topic and report what they learn. About how many mountain lions are still alive? In what states are they located? Can they be hunted or are they protected?

Endangered Savannah Animals

by Dave Taylor
New York: Crabtree, 1993. 32p.

This is a large-format book with excellent color photographs and will be enjoyed by readers in grades three through five.

There is a section on the African savannah and another on the problems of preserving the savannah. This large section of land in Africa is one of the world's richest habitats for wild animals. It contains both grassy areas and clumps of trees. Some animals prefer the wooded parts, some the grassy areas, and others, like the elephant and vulture, live in both. Animals' habitats are in danger because much of the land is being used as farmland. Animals are increasingly confined to game reserves and national parks. Poaching still occurs even though there are laws against it.

Among the animals described are: sable antelope, gerenuk, giraffes, Cape buffalo, black rhinoceros, zebras, African elephants, leopards, lions, and vultures. There is also a glossary and an index.

Students will enjoy reading and learning more about familiar African animals and may be especially intrigued by unusual ones. One lesser known animal discussed in the book is the gerenuk, which has the body and coloring of an antelope combined with the long neck of the giraffe. It is a member of the gazelle family and feeds on the leaves of over eighty kinds of trees.

Possible Topics for Further Investigation

1. The leopard's spotted coat offers perfect camouflage in the shadowy cover of the forests. Many other animals also make use of special coloration or camouflage. Invite a small group of interested students, with the help of an adult volunteer or the media specialist, to identify other insects, birds, or animals that have special camouflage. Students should bring books or magazines showing pictures of some of these animals to share.

2. Several countries discussed include: South Africa, Somalia, Ethiopia, and Kenya. Invite a pair of students to make a large map of Africa and name the countries of that continent. They might clip pictures from magazines or draw the various savannah animals. Pin these to a bulletin board around the map. Use yarn to connect a pin by each animal's picture to a pin on the map showing where it can be found.

3. The gerenuk looks like a "combination animal." It appears to have the body of an antelope and the neck of a giraffe. Students might enjoy making a picture book that can be bound and shared with a kindergarten class. Each student can add a page to the book that is a picture of a "combination animal" along with a caption giving its name. For example, there might be a hippo-giraf. Such an animal might have a giraffe's long neck and head attached to the chunky body of a hippopotamus. The rhino-skunk could have the horned head of a rhino attached to a skunk's striped body and tail.

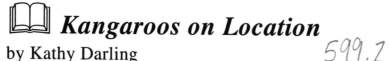

Kangaroos on Location

by Kathy Darling

Photographs by Tara Darling

New York: Lothrop, Lee & Shepard, 1993. 40p.

**NONFICTION
CONNECTIONS**

This book is illustrated with color photographs and will be enjoyed by students in grades two through five. The book is divided into five chapters, followed by a section called Kangaroo Facts and an index.

Chapter 1, "The Wonder Down Under," describes what it might have been like to be the first European explorers to arrive in Australia and see strange hopping creatures that we now call kangaroos. There are sixty different kinds of kangaroos and twelve close relatives called rat kangaroos. They are native only to Australia and nearby islands. Different kinds of kangaroos include wallaby, wallaroo, pademelon, euro, and forester.

Readers may be surprised to learn that kangaroos not only bound across open plains, but some climb trees, run through snow tunnels, swim in lakes, and leap off cliffs.

Chapter 2, "Bigfoot," describes how the dingo, or wild dog, is the only real threat to large kangaroos. This chapter also describes the recycled energy that allows kangaroos to jump great distances and the way in which they "punt" or walk.

Chapter 3, "Baby Factories," explains how kangaroos reproduce, and chapter 4, "Food Stuff," describes the way in which these animals consume huge quantities of green plants to stay alive. Chapter 5, "Survival Experts," explains how kangaroos have adapted to very dry conditions.

Possible Topics for Further Investigation

1   If students have been studying a variety of different animals, a group of them might wish to write questions for the class to solve. These questions will incorporate unusual facts about animals that the students have been studying. One question, for example, might be, "What animals never drink water even when it is available?" The answer would be *rock wallabies*. Students might want to write their questions on one side of a card with the answer on the other. When they have enough questions, students could divide the class into teams and hold an animal quiz show.

2   The art teacher might be willing to help a small group of students work with chicken wire and papier-mâché to create a class kangaroo. First, the students shape the wire into the form of an adult kangaroo. Then the students papier-mâché the form and, finally, paint it. The class kangaroo can be made big enough to hold a wastepaper basket as its "pouch." This will make classroom cleanup time fun!

3   Since kangaroos are only found in Australia and its nearby islands, a pair of students may enjoy making a salt-and-flour map for the classroom. The students should label Australia, Rottnest Island, Kangaroo Island, and Tasmania. On the continent of Australia, students should also indicate the Crater National Park, Planet Downs Ranch, Rockhampton, and Green Mountains—mentioned in this book. Using symbols, students could indicate where the different kinds of kangaroos are found.

From *Exploring the World of Animals.* © 1997. Teacher Ideas Press. (800) 237-6124.

Lion

by Caroline Arnold
New York: Morrow Junior Books, 1995. 48p.

This book is illustrated with color photographs taken at Wildlife Safari in Winston, Oregon, and supplemented with a few pictures taken in the wild. It will appeal to students in grades three through five.

Lions are known as king of the beasts. They live in groups, or prides, with the females leading in the hunt. Visitors can see and learn about lions by observing a pride of African lions that live in a wild animal park in southern Oregon. This book follows the lives of two cubs born in the animal park. The male cubs are named Keno and Tsavo, born to Sheeba.

These lions, and others in the pride, live in a large grassy area where they have room to move. They also have dens, which provide shelter at night and in cold or rainy weather. Visitors can drive through the lion enclosure and watch the animals through the closed windows of their vehicles.

The text notes that in the wild these lions would live on the grassland and open woodland of Africa, south of the Sahara Desert. Some wild lions also live in India.

Lions are members of the cat family, which is divided into three groups—the big cats, small cats, and the cheetah. A fourth group, the saber-toothed cats, are extinct.

The text gives information on the specialized eyes and feet of lions and explains how lions hunt, eat, drink, groom themselves, rest, roar, and grow up.

Possible Topics for Further Investigation

1   As king of the beasts, lions are at the top of the food chain. Introducing the concept of a food chain can be done in many different ways. One way is to dissect an owl pellet. Many biological supply companies sell owl pellet kits for classroom study. These can be used to study the diet of one predator. Within the pellet, students will be able to detect small limb bones from many different prey species.

2   One group of cats, the saber-toothed tigers, is now extinct. This might be an excellent time to have a small group of students prepare and display a geological time chart. Across the top of their chart, students could label four columns—era, period, epoch, and millions of years ago. A fifth column might be added in which the students could draw a picture showing a representative creature of that time period. The eras should include the Cenozoic, Mesozoic, and Paleozoic. The saber-toothed tiger, for example, would be shown as an example of a creature from the Cenozoic era, during the Tertiary period, in the recent Oligocene epoch.

3   The text mentions that all lions belong to the same species, *Panthera leo*. Most lions live in Africa, but a few live in Asia. An estimated 200 Asian lions live in the Gir Forest in India and are protected. Invite a pair of interested students, working with a media specialist, to find and report what they can learn about Asian lions. Why are there so few? Is their population growing or still dwindling?

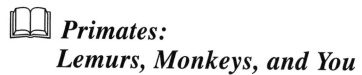

📖 *Primates:*
Lemurs, Monkeys, and You

by Ian Tattersall
Brookfield, CT: Millbrook Press, 1995. 72p.

This chapter book has a substantial amount of text and is illustrated with color drawings and photographs. It will be enjoyed by students in grades four and five. There is a glossary, index, and suggestions for further reading.

The text explains that there are over 200 species of primates living today. Primates have a five-fingered hand with an opposable thumb, and the fingers and toes are tipped by flat nails. Eyes have moved to the front of the head so that the field of vision of the two eyes overlap. Brains are fairly large and complex. Primates have a long period of development before birth and tend to live longer than most other mammals.

Modern primates are classified into two groups, prosimians and anthropoids. Prosimians alive today include lemurs, lorises and bushbabies, and tarsiers. The anthropoids include Old and New World monkeys, the lesser and greater apes, and humans.

New World monkeys are a diverse group that live in South and Central America. These primates are classified in the superfamily *Ceboidea*. Old World monkeys are divided into two groups. The *Cercopithecines* are found in Africa and Asia and in Gibraltar. They all have cheek pouches. The other major group is the colobine leaf monkeys. They live in Africa and Asia.

The earliest fossils known of a specifically human ancestor belong to *Australopithecus afarensis* that lived in Africa between three and four million years ago.

Possible Topics for Further Investigation

1   The introduction suggests an imaginary primate's party and describes the various "guests." A class bulletin board could be captioned "The Primate Party." Working in pairs, students can draw and add a picture of a primate mentioned in the introduction to the party. On an index card beneath each drawing, students should write the name of the animal and where it is found in the wild. Those pictured might include: a mouse lemur, a saucer-eyed night monkey, gorilla, patas monkey, proboscis monkey, colobus monkey, a sifaka, a gibbon, and a human.

2   One of the strangest of the primates discussed in this book is the aye-aye. A pair of students, with the help of a media specialist, might want to do some additional research on this animal, which is cat-sized with huge ears and enormous gnawing front teeth. Where is it found in the wild? Is it plentiful or endangered? What does it eat? What are its enemies? The students will want to share their research with classmates.

3   The glossary of this book contains some difficult vocabulary words. Students might want to use some of these words, and add others, to make a primate crossword puzzle. Using graph paper makes this task easier. Once words have been found to fit the puzzle spaces, clues or definitions should be included for the numbered words that go across or down. The finished puzzle and clues used might be duplicated and shared with the rest of the class members so that they might solve it.

📖 *Tiger, Tiger, Growing Up*

NONFICTION
CONNECTIONS

by Joan Hewett

New York: Clarion Books, 1993. 32p.

636.8
H497t

This large-format book has a minimum of text and is illustrated with color photographs. It will be enjoyed by students in grades two through four. Acknowledgments indicate that the photographs illustrating this book were taken at Marine World Africa USA, a wild animal park in Vallejo, California.

The book opens in the nursery at Marine World Africa where a week-old Bengal tiger is being fed a bottle of milk. The tiger's eyes have not opened yet. Tara was born in the park and was taken from her mother at five days old to be raised in the nursery. When Tara is nine days old, her eyes are open and she is given her first bath.

Because Tara needs feeding at night, Mary, one of her two trainers, takes the cub home with her and keeps her in a playpen in the house. She wakes just before each scheduled feeding. By three weeks, Tara has several teeth.

By the time Tara is three months old, she has been checked thoroughly by a vet and is ready to go with Lynn, her second trainer, to her first outdoor enclosure and walk around on a leash. Sometimes Tara is taken to classrooms to visit with children who learn that tigers are endangered animals.

At nine months, Tara gets new trainers who work with the park's adult tigers and she moves to her Tiger Island home. When she is fully grown at two to three years of age, Tara will weigh about 300 pounds.

Possible Topics for Further Investigation

1. Tara is a Bengal tiger. A pair of students might want to research Bengal and Siberian tigers to find similarities and differences between the two. How big does each grow? Where does each type of tiger live in the wild? (Students should be able to point out their natural home areas on a map.) Is their coloring different? In the wild, what types of food do they eat? What are their enemies? Student should report what they learn.

2. If there is a zoo near you, spring might be a perfect time for a class field trip. A pair of interested students might assist the teacher in making plans for the field trip. Phone calls and letters ahead of time will help ascertain if there is a zoo nursery, what animals are in it, when would be the best time for students to visit, and if there are special rates for school classes. Students might want to submit some of their questions about baby animals ahead of time. After the field trip the two students should follow up with a letter of thanks.

3. If you live near a zoo or animal park, the veterinarian who cares for the animals might be willing to make a school visit to discuss his or her work. Students might prepare questions ahead of time. Which animals require the most care from a vet and why? How can the vet work on animals that are big, strong, and dangerous? What was the veterinarian's most interesting patient? What kind of training does a zoo veterinarian need?

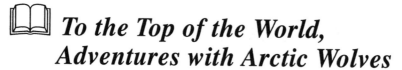

📖 *To the Top of the World, Adventures with Arctic Wolves*

by Jim Brandenburg
New York: Walker, 1993. 44p.

This book is illustrated with color photographs and will appeal to readers in grades three through five. It is written in first person by the author, who is also the photographer.

The book is presented in seven chapters. "The Ultimate Photograph" describes how the author, dressed in heavy arctic gear, follows a wolf to an iceberg and takes advantage of a shaft of light to catch a perfectly composed photograph of the wolf.

In "Meeting the Family," the readers learn more about the six wolf pups and seven adults who stay close to their den. Like a group of aunts, uncles, and parents, all are involved in caring for the young. Chapter 3, "Living as Neighbors," tells how the author sets up camp about a quarter of a mile from the wolf den.

Chapter 4, "Adaptation," describes the ways in which wolves sleep, curled into tight balls with their busy tails draped over their noses to protect them from the cold, and the shedding of the wolves' coats when warm weather approaches. It also tells of the ways they hunt caribou and hares and discusses their howling.

Chapter 5, "The Hunt," follows the wolves as they hunt for musk oxen, and Chapter 6, "Big Bad Wolves?," describes an incident in which the author moves a carcass that a wolf had been eating and is threatened by a wolf. The final chapter, "Good-Bye," tells how, accidentally, or on purpose, the wolf pack walks to the air strip and watches him board the plane the day that the author flies back to civilization.

Possible Topics for Further Investigation

1   This story takes place on Ellesmere Island near the Arctic Circle. Ask a small group of interested students to find out more about this remote spot. They should locate it on the map and research temperatures there during different months of the year, and the birds and animals that live there. These students should share what they learn.

2   At one point in the story, the wolves attack a herd of musk oxen. These are strange animals that are sometimes kept in commercial herds and raised for their fur, which is knitted into expensive scarves and hats. Qiviut is highly valued because of its warmth. Have a pair of interested students learn more about musk oxen. How and where do they live in the wild? How and where do they keep them for their fur? These students should write what they learn in a written report.

3   Shooting photographs of animals is a challenge. The author/photographer of this book is nationally acclaimed for his work. If students are interested, you might challenge them to enter a classroom "animal photography contest." Your contest rules may allow colored prints of pets as well as wild animals and birds. Set a deadline of six weeks to enter, with a maximum entry of three photos per student. Judges could be fellow staff members. An appropriate prize might be to mat and frame the winning photograph. (A frame shop owner might serve as a judge and also be willing to donate the matting and framing.)

Part V
Additional Resources

📖 Additional Fiction Titles 📖

Animals at Home

Barasch, Mara. *No Plain Pets.* New York: HarperCollins, 1991. 32p.

Blake, Robert J. *Dog.* New York: Philomel, 1994. 30p.

Boughton, Richard. *Rent-a-Puppy, Inc.* New York: Atheneum, 1992. 106p.

Fox, Paula. *One-Eyed Cat.* Scarsdale: Bradbury Press, 1984. 216p.

Hains, Harriet. *Our New Kitten.* New York: Dorling Kindersley, 1992. 21p.

Kushkin, Karla. *City Dog.* New York: Clarion, 1994. 30p.

Martin, Jerome. *Mitten/Kitten.* New York: Simon & Schuster, 1991. 34p.

Reisen, Lynn. *Any Kind of Dog.* New York: Greenwillow Books, 1992. 24p.

Roos, Stephen. *The Pet Lovers Club.* New York: Delacorte Press, 1992. 99p.

Schmeltz, Susan Alton. *Pets I Wouldn't Pick.* Milwaukee, WI: Gareth Stevens, 1993. 48p.

Animals on the Farm

Christelow, Eileen. *The Great Pig Escape.* New York: Clarion, 1994. 32p.

Henley, Claire. *Farm Day.* New York: Dial, 1991. 28p.

Herriot, James. *James Herriot's Treasury for Children.* New York: St. Martin's Press, 1992. 150p.

Kinsey-Warnock, Natalie. *When Spring Comes.* New York: Dutton, 1993. 30p.

Lewison, Wendy Cheyette. *Going to Sleep on the Farm.* New York: Dial, 1992. 32p.

Maddox, Tony. *Fergus's Upside Down Day.* Hauppage, NY: Barron's Educational Series, 1994. 28p.

Martin, C. L. G. *Down Dairy Farm Road.* New York: Macmillan, 1994. 32p.

McFarland, Cynthia. *Cows in the Parlor.* New York: Atheneum, 1990. 26p.

Tripp, Nathaniel. *Thunderstorm!* New York: Dial, 1994. 47p.

Ziefert, Harriet. *Oh, What a Noisy Farm.* New York: Tambourine Books, 1995. 28p.

Animals in the Woods

Bunting, Eve. *Red Fox Running*. New York: Clarion, 1993. 32p.

Burdick, Margaret. *Sara Raccoon and the Secret Place*. Boston: Little, Brown, 1992. 28p.

Coleman, Janet Wyman. *Fast Eddie*. New York: Four Winds Press, 1993. 128p.

Ernst, Lisa Campbell. *Squirrel Park*. New York: Bradbury Press, 1993. 30p.

Hiawyn, Oram. *Badger's Bring Something Party*. New York: Lothrop, Lee & Shepard, 1995. 26p.

Holmes, Efner Tucker. *Deer in the Hollow*. New York: Philomel, 1993. 32p.

Kasza, Keiko. *The Rat and the Tiger*. New York: G. P. Putnam's Sons, 1993. 32p.

Koertge, Ron. *Tiger, Tiger, Burning Bright*. New York: Orchard Books, 1994. 179p.

Mayo, Gretchen. *Meet Tricky Coyote!* New York: Walker, 1993. 36p.

Newman, Nanette. *There's a Bear in the Bath!* San Diego, CA: Harcourt Brace, 1994. 32p.

Animals in the Wild

Arnold, Marsha Diane. *Heart of a Tiger*. New York: Dial Books for Young Readers, 1995. 30p.

Borovsky, Paul. *Nico*. New York: Crown, 1993. 28p.

Campbell, Eric. *The Year of the Leopard Song*. San Diego, CA: Harcourt Brace, 1992. 161p.

Cavanagh, Helen. *Panther Glade*. New York: Simon & Schuster, 1993. 144p.

Couisins, Lucy. *Za-Za's Baby Brother*. Cambridge, MA: Candlewick Press, 1995. 26p.

Franklin, Kristine L. *When the Monkeys Came Back*. New York: Atheneum, 1994. 30p.

Landsman, Sandy. *Castaways on Chimp Island*. New York: Atheneum, 1986. 202p.

Paul, Anthony. *The Tiger Who Lost His Stripes*. San Diego, CA: Harcourt Brace, 1995. 32p.

Thaler, Mike. *Come and Play, Hippo*. New York: HarperCollins, 1991. 62p.

Vyner, Sue. *Arctic Spring*. New York: Viking, 1992. 30p.

📖 Additional Nonfiction Titles 📖

Animals at Home

Alderton, David. *Dogs, The Visual Guide to Over 300 Dog Breeds from Around the World*. New York: Dorling Kindersley, 1993. 304p.

Burton, Jane. *Kitten*. New York: Lodestar, 1991. 21p.

Evans, Mark. *Hamster*. New York: Dorling Kindersley, 1993. 45p.

Hansen, Elvig. *Guinea Pigs*. Minneapolis, MN: Carolrhoda Books, 1992. 48p.

Patent, Dorothy Hinshaw. *Hugger to the Rescue*. New York: Cobblehill, 1994. 31p.

Piers, Helen. *Taking Care of Your Cat*. Hauppauge, NY: Barron's Educational Series, 1992. 32p.

Wadsworth, Ginger. *Susan Butcher, Sled Dog Racer*. Minneapolis, MN: Lerner, 1994. 63p.

Wexler, Jerome. *Pet Hamsters*. Morton Grove, IL: Albert Whitman, 1992. 47p.

Ziefert, Harriet. *Let's Get a Pet*. New York: Viking, 1993. 32p.

Animals on the Farm

Clayton, Gordon. *Lamb*. New York: Lodestar, 1992. 21p.

Epstein, Sam. *You Call That a Farm?* New York: Farrar, Straus Giroux, 1991. 63p.

Hopkins, Lee Bennett. *On the Farm: Poems*. Boston: Little, Brown, 1991. 32p.

James, Shirley Kerby. *Going to a Horse Farm*. Watertown, MA: Charlesbridge, 1992. 30p.

Manci, William E. *Farming and the Environment*. Milwaukee, WI: Gareth Stevens, 1993. 32p.

McGregor, Meredeth. *Cowgirl*. New York: Walker, 1992. 28p.

Morris, Ann. *700 Kids on Grandpa's Farm*. New York: Dutton, 1994. 32p.

Patent, Dorothy Hinshaw. *Where Food Comes From*. New York: Holiday House, 1991. 40p.

Sanchez, Isidro. *The Farm*. New York: Barron's Educational Series, 1991. 31p.

Warren, Jean. *ABC Farm*. Everett, WA: Warren, 1991. 43p.

Animals in the Woods

Haas, Jessie. *Chipmunk!* New York: Greenwillow Books, 1993. 32p.

Johnston, Ginny. *Windows on Wildlife.* New York: Morrow Junior Books, 1990. 48p.

Kalbacken, Joan. *White-tailed Deer.* Chicago: Childrens Press, 1992. 45p.

Lepthien, Emile U. *Foxes.* Chicago: Childrens Press, 1993. 44p.

Patent, Dorothy Hinshaw. *Deer and Elk.* New York: Clarion Books, 1994. 77p.

Robinson, Sandra Chisholm. *Mountain Lion.* Denver, CO: Denver Museum of Natural History, 1991. 62p.

Ryden, Hope. *The Raggedy Red Squirrel.* New York: Dutton, 1992. 32p.

Schlein, Miriam. *Squirrel Watching.* New York: HarperCollins, 1992. 64p.

Stone, Lynn M. *Skunks.* Vero Beach, FL: Rourke, 1990. 24p.

Tomblin, Gill. *Small & Furry Animals: A Watercolor Sketchbook of Mammals in the Wild.* New York: Putnam & Grosset Book Group, 1992. 61p.

Animals in the Wild

Arnold, Caroline. *Monkey.* New York: Morrow Junior Books, 1993. 48p.

Arnold, Caroline. *Rhino.* New York: Morrow Junior Books, 1995. 48p.

Cooper, Ann C. *The Wildwatch Book.* Niwot, CO: Roberts Rhinehart, 1990. 90p.

George, Dick. *Ruby: The Painting Pachyderm of the Phoenix Zoo.* New York: Delacorte Press, 1995. 48p.

Grace, Eric S. *Apes.* San Francisco: Sierra Club Books, 1995. 64p.

Irvine, Georgeanne. *Blanca and Arusha: Tales of Two Big Cats.* New York: Simon & Schuster, 1995. 45p.

Lindbad, Lisa. *The Serengeti Migration: Africa's Animals on the Move.* New York: Hyperion, 1994. 40p.

Redmond, Ian. *Gorilla.* New York: Knopf, 1995. 63p.

Stone, Lynn M. *Hyenas.* Vero Beach, FL: Rourke, 1990. 24p.

Tibbitts, Allison. *Koalas.* Mankato, MN: Capstone Press, 1992. 32p.

Magazines and Videorecordings
of Possible Interest

Magazines

Chickade
Young Naturalist Foundation
P.O. Box 11314
Des Moines, IA 50340

Owl
Young Naturalist Foundation
P.O. Box 11314
Des Moines, IA 50340

National Geographic World
National Geographic Society
P.O. Box 2330
Washington, DC 20013-9865

Ranger Rick
National Wildlife Federation
8925 Leesburg Pike
Vienna, VA 22184-0001

Videorecordings

The Alphabet Zoo. Allen, TX: Barney Home Video, 1993. Videocassette, 30 min.

Antlers Big and Small. Bethesda, MD: Discovery Enterprises, 1991. Videocassette, 25 min.

Babes in the Woods. Bethesda, MD: Discovery Enterprises, 1992. Videocassette, 25 min.

Bear Cubs, Baby Ducks, and Kooky Kookaburras. Burbank, CA: Columbia Tristar Home Video, 1994. Videocassette, 33 min.

The Business of Beavers. Bethesda, MD: Discovery Enterprises, 1991. Videocassette, 25 min.

Cougar. Stamford, CT: Capital Cities/ABC Video Publishing, 1990. Videocassette, 50 min.

Cranberry Bounce. Bellingham, WA: De Beck Educational Video, 1991. Videocassette, 30 min.

Living with the Elk. Sheridan, WY: Grunko Films, 1993. Videocassette, 55 min.

The Search for Canada's Most Secret Animal. Edison, NJ: Fox/Lorber Associates, 1990. Videocassette, 30 min.

Wolves. Los Angeles, CA: Vestron Video, 1992. Videocassette, 60 min.

Zebra. Washington, DC: National Geographic Video, Columbus Tristar Home Video, 1991. Videocassette, 60 min.

Author-Title Index

ABOUT THE AUTHOR

Phyllis J. Perry has worked as a teacher, an elementary school principal, a district curriculum specialist, a supervisor of student teachers, and as Director of Talented and Gifted Education. She is the author of more than two dozen books for children and teachers including seven First Books for Franklin Watts and the Literature Bridges to Science series for Teacher Ideas Press.

Dr. Perry received her undergraduate degree from the University of California at Berkeley and her doctorate from the University of Colorado in Boulder. She now devotes full time to writing and lives with her husband, David, in Boulder, Colorado.

from **Teacher Ideas Press**

Of Bugs and Beasts: Fact, Folklore, and Activities
Lauren J. Livo, Glenn McGlathery, and Norma J. Livo

Intriguing profiles of nature's least-loved animals—bats, snakes, coyotes, leeches, skunks, slugs, toads—reveal their beneficial qualities, their vital roles in the ecosystem, and their overlooked but inherent natural grandeur. **All Levels**.
Learning Through Folklore Series; Norma J. Livo, Ed.
xxi, 217p. 8½x11 paper ISBN 1-56308-179-2

Investigating Science Through Bears
Karlene Ray Smith and Anne Hudson Bush

Introduce students to one of nature's most endearing animals and inspire learning across the curriculum with a delightful diversity of activities focusing on bears. Historical anecdotes, recipes, songs, a bibliography of resources, and more offer unique and stimulating experiences that you and your students will treasure for a lifetime.
Grades 2–5.
xvi, 211p. 8½x11 paper ISBN 1-56308-072-9

Science Through Children's Literature: An Integrated Approach
Carol M. Butzow and John W. Butzow

This best-seller provides instructional units that integrate all areas of the curriculum and serve as models to educators at all levels. Adopted by schools of education nationwide, it features more than 30 outstanding children's fiction books that are rich in scientific concepts yet equally well known for their strong story lines and universal appeal.
Grades K–3.
xviii, 234p. 8½x11 paper ISBN 0-87287-667-5

Primary Dinosaur Investigations: How We Know What We Know
Craig A. Munsart and Karen Alonzi Van Gundy

Take students from a fascination with dinosaurs to science success with delightful dinosaur-based activities that teach them to think like scientists. This introductory teachers' guide is packed with classroom-ready, teacher-friendly, student-tested activities that will engage students and help them develop critical-thinking and research skills. **Grades K–3**.
xxi, 293p. 8½x11 paper ISBN 1-56308-246-2

Nature at Your Doorstep: Real World Investigations for Primary Students
Carole G. Basile, Fred Collins, Jennifer Gillespie-Malone

Share the wonder of nature with young learners while building scientific knowledge and skills! Engaging activities guide learning about birds, habitats, biodiversity, and other topics into the study of all major areas of ecology. Students can perform the simple projects right in their own backyards (or school yards)! **Grades K–3**.
xxvi, 161p. 8½x11 paper ISBN 1-56308-455-4

Beyond the Bean Seed: Gardening Activities for Grades K–6
Nancy Allen Jurenka and Rosanne J. Blass

Engaging book-based lessons integrate gardening, children's literature, and language arts through creative activities embellished with poetry, word play, and recipes. The projects lead to learning in a variety of other subjects—from ecology, history, and geography to career exploration and the sciences. **Grades K–6**.
xiv, 195p. 8½x11 paper ISBN 1-56308-346-9

For a FREE catalog or to order any of our titles, please contact:
Teacher Ideas Press
Dept. B25 • P.O. Box 6633 • Englewood, CO 80155-6633
Phone: 1-800-237-6124 • Fax: 303-220-8843 • E-mail: lu-books@lu.com